MORE
WEIRD AND
WONDERFUL
WORDS

SPANGHEW

spanghew [**spang**-hyoo] to cause a frog or toad to fly into the air. (Usually violently, from the end of a stick, although it seems as though it wouldn't ever feel gentle to the poor toad or frog!) Of obscure origin.

MORE WEIRD AND WONDERFUL WORDS

EDITED BY
Erin McKean

ILLUSTRATIONS BY
Danny Shanahan

WITH A FOREWORD BY RICHARD LEDERER

OXFORD
UNIVERSITY PRESS
2003

OXFORD
UNIVERSITY PRESS

Oxford   New York

Auckland   Bangkok   Buenos Aires   Cape Town   Chennai
Dar es Salaam   Delhi   Hong Kong   Istanbul   Karachi   Kolkata
Kuala Lumpur   Madrid   Melbourne   Mexico City   Mumbai   Nairobi
São Paulo   Shanghai   Singapore   Taipei   Tokyo   Toronto

Copyright © 2003 by Oxford University Press, Inc.

Published by Oxford University Press, Inc.
198 Madison Avenue, New York, NY 10016-4314
http://www.oup.com

Library of Congress Cataloging-in-Publication Data
More weird and wonderful words / edited by Erin McKean ;
illustrations by Danny Shanahan ; with a foreword by Richard Lederer.
p. cm.
Includes bibliographical references.
ISBN 0-19-517057-1 (hardcover : alk. paper)
1. Vocabulary. I. McKean, Erin. II. Shanahan, Danny.
PE1449.M625 2003
428.1—dc21   2003011540

The essay "Finding New Weird and Wonderful Words" was previously published in
slightly different form in *The Oxford Essential Dictionary of New Words*, Berkley, 2003.

Designed by Nora Wertz

9 8 7 6 5 4 3 2 1

Printed in the United States of America
on acid-free paper

TABLE OF CONTENTS

For Joey and Henry

E. M.

For Finnegan

D. S.

# FOREWORD

When I was a boy, I played with those small winged thingumabobs that grow on—and contain the seeds of—maple trees. I glued them to my nose and watched them spin like pinwheels when I tossed them into the wind. Only as a grownup did I discover that these organic whatchamacallits do have a name—*schizocarps*. So do the uglifying fleshy growths on a turkey's face (a *snood*) and the heavy flaps on the sides of the mouths of some dogs (*flews*). So do all sorts of human body parts that you never thought had names: *canthus, cerumen, frenulum, opisthenar, philtrum, thenar, tragus, uvula,* and *vomer*.

Name givers of the past have designated the half-smoked plug of tobacco in a pipe bowl as *dottle*, the decaying matter on a forest floor as *duff*, the holder for a paper cone coffee cup a *zarf*, and the slit made when one starts to saw a piece of wood as the *kerf*.

Ever since Adam assigned names to all the animals, we human beings have managed to come up with labels for almost everything on this planet—and beyond. Many of these names are so obscure that no one except dictionary editors knows them. The rest of us are reduced to referring to these things with words that mean "that object I don't know the name for." We have managed to come up with more than thirty ways of signifying that for which we don't have a name, including *doohickey, gigamaree, thingumajog, whatchamacallit,* and, as you'll soon discover in this book, *curwhibble. More Weird and Wonderful Words* provides a remedy for that tongue-tangled state. It will help you fill in the semantic holes of all those doohickeys and whatchamacallits and brush bursting color onto the patches of blank space in your picture of the world.

According to the Mayan sacred book *Popol Vuh,* after the Creators had made the earth, carved it with mountains, valleys, and rivers, and covered it with vegetation, they formed the animals who would be guardians of the plant world and who would praise the Makers' names: "'Speak, then, our names, praise us, your mother, your father. Invoke, then, Huracan, Chipi-Caculha, the Heart of Heaven, the Heart of Earth, the Creator, the Maker, the Forefathers. Speak, invoke us, adore us.' But the animals only hissed and screamed and cackled. They were unable to make words, and each screamed in a different way. When the Creator and the Maker saw that it was impossible for them to talk to each other, they said: 'It is impossible for them to say the names of us, their Creators and Makers. This is not well.' As a punishment, the birds and animals were condemned to be eaten and sacrificed by others, and the Creators set out to make another creature who would be able to call their names and speak their praises. This creature was man and woman."

In biblical Genesis, we read that God said, "Let us make man in our image, after our likeness." As in the Mayan myth of creation, God bestowed upon human beings the power of language, the power to name things: "And out of the ground the Lord God formed every beast of the field, and every fowl of the air; and brought them unto Adam to see what he would call them: and whatsoever Adam called every living creature, that was the name thereof. And Adam gave names to all cattle, and to the fowl of the air, and to every beast of the field."

The human passion and power to name everything is nowhere better demonstrated than in our ability to label almost everything we encounter. Through the wabe of our word-bethumped English language gyre and gimble as many as two million words, the most Brobdingnagian vocabulary by far in the history of humankind. Such a wealth of words creates a case of inconspicuous nonconsumption. Thousands of vibrant but no longer vibrating English words lie unused in arcane crannies of huge or obscure dictionaries and end up buried in the boneyards of obsolescence. Erin McKean has spent years sweeping out the dusty corners of dictionaries. She has exhumed her weird and wonderful words from obsolete and nearly forgotten graves because in her judgment they have been untimely ripped from our vocabularies and deserve another chance to live. There are more words, Horatio, than are dreamt of in your philosophy.

You probably don't know that a single word can describe the rosy light of dawn, the cooing of doves, the art of writing in the dark, or (in the manner of Georges Simenon and Isaac Asimov) the act of continuous writing, but those words—*rosicler, roucoulement, scoteography,* and *scriptitation*—have a new home in the pages of this book. Are you, like me, a water drinker and booze shunner? Then you are, in a word, an *aquabib.* Do you, like Shaquille O'Neal and me, have large feet? You are, in another word, *scipodous.* Perhaps Macbeth and his hen-pecking, buzzard-battering lady would have lived and ended their lives less bloodily if they had known that they were both *dretched.*

Here, too, reposes a superb opportunity to insult your enemies with impunity. By creatively combining selected entries of disparagement, you can brand your nemesis a *badot battologist,* a *foisonless cumber-ground,* a *furciferous zizany,* a *balatronic hoddypeak,* a *trichechine jollux,* an *infrendiate volpone,* a *scolecophagous stafador,* a *drumbling gilly-gaupus,* or a *scelestious, roinish, uliginous drazel.*

O *impigrous, illecebrous, isangelous, leggiadrous, peramene, swasivious, viscerotonic* reader, after you have explored this book, please reread the previous paragraph to realize fully the inventive invective of which our English language is capable, and please reread this sentence to see what subtle compliments we possess the potential to bestow.

Remembrance of words past also raises the art of the euphemism to its loftiest stratum. You don't always have to call a spade a spade. That's not a double chin you sport, it's a *choller.* If you are fixated on the care and maintenance of your hair, you are not narcissistic; you are, more mysteriously and less judgmentally, *philocomal.* If you have a friend who used to share your interests but—weep weep, sob sob—no longer does, he or she evidences *ageustia,* the loss of the sense of taste. If your relatives are bugging you about your state of singlehood, explain that you are happy to be *agamous,* and they may come to share your joy.

Then there is the crackling logophony of many of the words in this book, words that tingle around the tongue, ricochet off the teeth and palate, and shoot from the mouth like a watermelon seed. You'll encounter the definitions of all these ear-rinsing words in the pages ahead, but for now simply allow yourself to be merged with the collide-o-scope of their sounds: *Bogglish. Camstairy. Flambuginous.*

Impluvious. Infrendiate. Jirble. Kakistocracy. Rixation. Sardoodledom. Whistness. Winx. Zizany.

Trust me. It's not *inaniloquent morology* and *balbutiating galimatias* driveling from my fingertips massaging the keyboard when I tell you that *More Weird and Wonderful Words* demonstrates that there are lots of things and ideas in the universe that actually do have names, even though hardly anybody knows them. Spotted owls, snail darters, and whales are not the only treasures on our endangered list these days. Scores of our most colorful and precise words are on the verge of extinction after generations of service. Fortunately, these specimens of logodiversity find refuge and rejuvenation in Erin McKean's wild-word sanctuary. Lexicographers like McKean are not harmless drudges. Rather, they remind us of the unbounded generativity of our glorious, uproarious, outrageous, courageous, tremendous, stupendous, end-over-endous English language.

Richard Lederer,
San Diego, California

 # INTRODUCTION

In the introduction to *Weird and Wonderful Words,* I wrote:

What makes a word weird? It would be convenient to say that it's as ineffable as whatever it is that makes art Art, but that's not quite true. Words are weird because they have odd sounds, or an abundance of syllables, or a completely gratuitous *k, j, q, z,* or *x*. Words are often weird because they mean something weird. They let you see, for as long as you care to dwell on them, some of the truly bizarre things that people have had, done, used, invented, feared, or thought.

What makes a word wonderful *is* ineffable. It has to hit you like a good joke, or a satisfying denouement, or the scent of something tantalizing in the air. It makes you want to go off on tangents, or rants, or wild goose chases. It adds something, not just to your vocabulary (since you may never even speak or write any of these wonderful words), but to your being. Like anything wonderful (to abuse etymology), it fills you with wonder. It opens vistas.

There are plenty of words that are weird without being the least bit wonderful—*nectocalyx* is orthographically weird, but meaning as it does 'the swimming-bell that forms the natatory organ in many hydrozoans' it is sadly lacking on the wonder scale. There are wonderful words, such as *brio* and *luminescent*, which long familiarity has deprived of any weirdness. Finding a truly weird and wonderful word is like meeting a gorgeous person who is also a good cook and will help you move.

When I wrote those words, I'd found more than four hundred weird and wonderful words. And in this book, just a few pages from here, there are more than four hundred more. It seems (luckily for us) that weird and wonderful words are a renewable resource. The mine has not played out, nor the well dried up; new candidates for the *Weird and Wonderful* seal of approval, both ancient and newly minted, are constantly coming to light. Quite a few of the words in this book were passed along to me by folks sharing their own treasures; weird words are one of the few things that you can simultaneously give away and keep for yourself.

We've also had the good luck to be able to share these words with Danny Shanahan, who has returned them to us transformed into (and often surprisingly combined in) wonderfully twisted and bizarre cartoons.

Tremendous thanks to Martin Coleman, for managing the project (without actually making us *feel* managed), Connie Baboukis and Enid Pearsons for performing stupendous feats of orthoepy, Carol-June Cassidy for keeping a stern guiding hand on our relative pronouns, Nora Wertz for another ebullient design, and Casper Grathwohl for enthusiasm, mad accounting skillz, and sympathy.

Pronunciation note: We've added pronunciations for the words in this book, pronunciations that we hope are straightforward. The tricky bits: an underlined th is the *th* sound in *bathe*. **Boldface** indicates a stressed syllable. And, because many of these words have not been sounded by human voices for centuries, all pronunciations are for entertainment purposes only.

MORE
WEIRD AND
WONDERFUL
WORDS

ablegate [**ab**-li-git] a representative of the pope who brings a newly named cardinal his insignia of office. *Ablegate* is a much more impressive title than *Hiring Manager*.

abligurition [ab-lig-yoo-**rish**-un] the spending of an unconscionable amount on food. This comes from a Latin word meaning 'to spend freely and indulgently on luxuries', which was itself derived from another Latin word meaning 'to lick'.

abnormous [ab-**nor**-mus] a word that looks recently and slangily made-up, but was in fact slangily made-up in about 1742. It means 'misshapen'.

acrasia [uh-**kray**-zhuh] the state of mind in which you act against your better judgment; lack of self-control. From a Greek word meaning 'no strength'. Another helpful and obfuscating word to hide weakness; this time good for dieters.

acrophony [ack-**krah**-fuh-nee] the use of a picture to communicate a sound. From Greek words meaning 'highest' and 'voice'. The initial sound or syllable of the name of the pictured object is usually the one intended.

agalaxy [ag-uh-**lack**-see] lack of milk after childbirth. This is same *galaxy* as the starry one; both come from a Greek word meaning 'milk'. Lack of milk for a child and lack of stars seem, in a mother's mind, to be equal catastrophes.

agamous [ag-uh-mus] an adjective meaning 'unmarried'. Useful for single people with nagging relatives. "I'm happy being *agamous*, really, Aunt Mabel" will have them convinced of your alternative lifestyle (not that there's anything wrong with that) and with any luck head off further inquiry. Just hope that a more motivated and worried relative doesn't skip down in the dictionary to a further meaning: 'without distinguishable sexual organs'. This much more disturbing meaning is used mostly about plants—*cryptogamous* is the word more commonly used. *Agamous* comes from a Greek word of the same meaning.

ageustia [ug-**yoo**-stee-uh] the loss of the sense of taste. Could be extended in nonmedical use for someone who used to share your interests but for some reason has now sadly morphed into someone who does not.

aginate [**adj**-uh-nate] to sell small things. The noun *aginator* would be a nice term for an online auction seller. "Oh, I'm an *aginator* on eBay, you know." The citation in the *OED* gives the gloss "He which retaileth," from 1626. From a Latin word for a part of a scale.

agiotage [**adj**-uh-tidj] maneuvering by speculators to raise or lower the price of stocks or funds. From a French word of the same spelling meaning 'stockjobbing'. The first citation given in the *OED* for this word is "Vanity and *agiotage* are to a Parisian the oxygen and hydrogen of life," by Walter Savage Landor, from his best-known work (which is not saying much), *Imaginary Conversations*.

AGINATOR

FINNIMBRUNS
50¢

agist [uh-**jist**] to put a public burden on private lands. Originally landholders along a coast were charged for the coastguard protecting them. This could be extended to include any tax or charge that falls upon users of a public service. From an Old French word meaning 'to lodge'. Another meaning of the word was essentially 'to give room and board to cattle'. The *agistor* (or *agister*) was an officer of the royal forests who took charge of cattle *agisted* there and accounted for the money paid for their *agistment*.

agogic [uh-**gah**-jick] an adjective meaning 'of or about the making of wax models'. Sadly, this word is nowhere to be found on the website of the Madame Tussaud's museums.

agonous [**ag**-uh-nus] obviously related to *agony* and *agonize*, this word's meaning hasn't yet been watered down: it means 'struggling, engaged in mortal combat'.

agrapha [**ag**-ruh-fuh] the collective name for sayings attributed to Jesus but not recorded in the canonical Gospels. This would also be a nice collective term for those quotations that "everybody knows was said by ____" but are, in fact, sadly apocryphal, such as "Elementary, my dear Watson, elementary," (which never appears in any Holmes book but is instead found in *Psmith, Journalist* by P. G. Wodehouse!). *Agrapha* comes from a Greek word meaning 'not written'.

anopisthograph [an-oh-**pis**-thoh-graf] something that has writing on only one side (usually paper, although you could pedantically use this for things like T-shirts or billboards). *Anopisthography* is the practice of writing on only one side of something, a policy disdained by those who know how to make that 1→2 button on the copy machine work. (*Opisthography* is the practice of writing on both sides.) From Greek words that mean 'written on the back or cover'.

antonomasia [an-tuh-noh-**may**-zee-uh] the practice, abhorred by lawyers, of using a trademark (like Kleenex or Xerox) as a generic term. From Greek words meaning 'against' and 'to name'. If this is done often enough (and the owners of the trademark do not protest enough) the word may become generic, as happened with *thermos* and *aspirin*.

SLANGREL AVETROL GANGREL

aquabib [**ack**-wuh-bib]   a water drinker. Someone hated by bartenders and waiters everywhere.

avetrol [**av**-uh-trawl]   a bastard. Possibly related to a Latin word meaning 'to debauch, to corrupt', bastards for centuries being thought of as a natural consequence of debauchery.

badot [bad-**doh**] a rare and obsolete adjective meaning 'silly'. From a French word meaning 'a gaping idler'.

baetyl [**bee**-tle] a sacred meteoric stone. These stones were thought to have life, and were sometimes set up underneath holy trees.

baisemain [bez-**man**] an obsolete word meaning 'a kiss on the hand', and, by extension, 'compliments'. From a French word of the same meaning.

baithe [ba**the**] a rare and obsolete word meaning 'to agree, to consent'. From an Old Norse word meaning 'to beg'.

balatronic [bal-uh-**trah**-nik] an adjective meaning 'of or pertaining to buffoons'. The citation in the *OED* refers to "students of the *balatronic* dialect [who keep] an interleaved copy of the Slang Dictionary." For research purposes, only, of course. From a Latin word meaning 'babbler'.

balbutiate [bal-**byoo**-shee-ate] to stutter or stammer. From a Latin word meaning 'to stammer'. Someone who is *balbutient* is stammering. *Balbuties* is the medical term for stuttering or lisping, or, as one citation has it, "vicious pronunciation."

ballotade [bal-uh-**tayd**] a kind of jump in which a horse bends all four legs without kicking out the hind ones. (No animals were injured in the writing of this definition.) From a French word meaning 'a small ball'. Another word from this root is *ballottement*, a way of diagnosing pregnancy, where the front of the uterus is pushed suddenly and the fetus is felt to move away and back again. It would seem most pregnancies would be fairly apparent by the time this method was effective.

BANGSTRY

bangstry [**bang**-stree] an obsolete and rare word meaning 'masterful violence'. It would be nice to survey bodice-ripper novels to see if this appears anywhere, masterful violence being something of a bodice-ripper trope.

barathrum [**barr**-uh-thrum] a deep pit in Athens, into which condemned criminals were thrown to die. There are as yet no *barathrums* in Texas. Also, any pit or abyss.

barla-fumble [**bahr**-luh **fum**-ble] a call for a time-out or truce by someone who has fallen while playing or wrestling. From *parley*, 'truce'.

battologist [bat-**tah**-luh-djist] someone who repeats the same thing needlessly. From a Greek word meaning 'stammerer'.

bifilar [bye-**fye**-ler] having two threads or using two threads. Most modern sewing machines are *bifilar* (or even *tri*- or *quatrifilar*). Early sewing machines weren't—they were trying to reproduce mechanically *monofilar* handsewing, unsuccessfully—and it wasn't until 1833 that an American Quaker, Walter Hunt, invented the first *bifilar* sewing machine. (Unfortunately, it couldn't sew curved seams, so it wasn't a success either.)

blennorrhea [blen-uh-**ree**-uh] an unusually large secretion and discharge of mucus. You know that any word ending in *-rrhea* is bound to be unpleasant, but this one is particularly so. Something (or an unfortunate someone) who is *blennogenous* generates mucus.

blive [bleev] an obsolete adverb that originally meant 'immediately, right away' but gradually came to mean 'before long, soon', just in the same way that "I'll be there in a second" means "I hope you have something to read while you wait."

bloncket [**blahng**-kit] gray, or a light grayish blue. It comes from a French word meaning 'whitish', and, like many whitish things, eventually became flat-out gray.

blottesque [blah-**tesk**] (of paintings) having blots or heavy brushwork, not finely done. A combination of *blot* and the *-esque* of *grotesque*. Not, as you might imagine, a complimentary term, it was first used by John Ruskin to criticize modern painting.

bogglish [**bahg**-glish] uncertain, doubtful, skittish. This is one of those words, which, if it did not exist, would have to be invented for the pure joy of the combination of letters and sounds. How nice to be able to say, "I'll have to get back to you about that, I'm a bit *bogglish*."

bombilation [bahm-buh-**lay**-shun] a buzzing, droning, or humming sound. This word sounds as if it should be much more severe than the definition strictly allows; if you had said you were kept awake by *bombilation* all night, it seems that rubble and sirens would be expected, not just somebody's overbassed car or a neighbor's TV.

bordlode [**bord**-lode] a service required of tenants, particularly the duty to carry firewood from the woods to the landlord's house. This makes the requirements of co-op and condo boards seem relatively reasonable.

brannigan [**bran**-ig-in] a rare word meaning 'a drinking bout, a spree or binge'. One of the citations in the *OED* is from H. L. Mencken's *American Mercury* magazine: "He may seek escape by going on prolonged crossword puzzle *brannigans*." You can sense Mencken's pleasure in contrasting a word like *brannigan* with such a sedentary occupation.

bubulcitate [buh-**bull**-si-tate] to cry like a cowboy, to work as a cowboy. (The cowboy meant here, of course, is more like *cowherd*, but it's funnier to think of it as a lonesome American cowboy.) From a Latin word meaning 'cowherd'.

bucculent [**buck**-yuh-lunt] an obsolete and rare word meaning 'wide-mouthed'. From a Latin word meaning 'cheek'.

bucentaur [byoo-**sen**-tawr] a large and improbably decorated barge, often one used for a state event. The first of the name may have been the one in which the Doges of Venice pledged their fidelity to the Adriatic Sea in a marriage ceremony on the feast of the Ascension every year. A *bucentaur* is also a half-man half-ox creature.

buchette [boo-**shett**] a rare and obsolete word meaning 'a piece of firewood'.

buffard [**buff**-erd] an obsolete and rare word meaning 'a fool'. Possibly from a French word meaning 'often puffing'.

bufo [**byoo**-foh] an obsolete word meaning 'the black tincture of the alchemists'. From a Latin word meaning 'toad'.

bullimong [**bull**-uh-mung] various grains all mixed together, used for feeding cattle. By extension, any heterogenous mess.

camstairy [kam-**stair**-ee] a Scots adjective meaning 'perverse, willful, or obstinate'. Possibly related to *cam*, 'crooked'.

canescent [kuh-**ness**-unt] hoary, grayish or dull white, like the hairs on the leaves of plants. Although this looks like it should be related to *canine*, it's from a Latin word meaning 'to grow hoary'. Perhaps it could be used to describe certain dinner-party stories, especially those related by one's spouse.

caphar [kaf-**fahr**] an obsolete word for the money paid for protection by Christian merchants taking merchandise to Jerusalem. From an Arabic word meaning 'defense'.

capilotade [kap-i-loh-**tahd**] a hashed-together story. From the name of a dish made of minced veal, chicken, capon, or partridge, separated by beds of cheese.

catoblephon [kat-uh-**bleff**-un] an unidentified African mammal described in the works of the ancients. Possibly a buffalo or a gnu, it was 'a creature like a bull, whose eyes are so fixed as chiefly to look downward'.

chairoplane [**chair**-uh-plane] a merry-go-round or carousel where the seats are suspended from chains, and the riders are swung outward in a circle as the center support goes around. Unfortunately, two of the citations in the *OED* have this word collocated with 'victim' and 'tragedy'. From *chair* plus the *plane* of *airplane*.

chamade [shuh-**mahd**] a signal inviting someone to a parley (usually a drumbeat or trumpet sounding). Now perhaps useful to those who have to carry beepers—"Sorry, have to go, it's a *chamade*."

chaston [**chas**-tun] the part of a ring that holds a stone (also called a *collet*).

chessom [**chess**-um] an adjective, usually used about soil, meaning 'without stones or grit'. No reason, though, why it couldn't be used for oysters and spinach.

chiliad [**kill**-ee-ad] a group of a thousand things, especially a period of a thousand years. (Since I discovered this word much too late to be of any use for the last turn-of-the-millennium, I have grandiose, Walt Disneyesque plans for making sure I have an opportunity to use it next time . . .)

choical [**koy**-i-cle] a Gnostic term, coming from a Greek word for 'dust'. The Gnostics believed that the visible body was made up of two parts: a "subtle element" that they called the *hylic body*, and a "sheath of gross earthly matter" that they called the *choical body*.

choil [koil] the name of the indented part of a pocketknife where the edge of the blade adjoins the tang or thick part by which it is hafted, or the corresponding part of any knife where the cutting edge ends. To *choil* is to make this indention or slope in a knife, and a *choiler* is an instrument for making the *choil*. The *OED* says, "*Choil* has been used in Sheffield from before the memory of the oldest inhabitant."

choller [**chah**-ler] a double chin, or the hanging lip of a hound dog.

concinnous [kun-**sin**-us] a neat and elegant adjective meaning 'neat, elegant'.

consuetudinary [kahns-wi-**t(y)oo**-duh-ner-ee] a guide to customs, rituals, or practices, especially those of a religious order.

corrade [kuh-**rade**] an obsolete word meaning 'to gather together from various sources'. From a Latin word meaning 'to scrape together'. One of the early citations (1619) from the *OED* makes the excuse of anthologists everywhere: "I haue made choise of mine Authors, not *corrading* out of all promiscue."

coshering [**kahsh**-er-ing] an obsolete and rare Irish word meaning 'feasting'. Also, the tradition among Irish chiefs of paying extended (and most likely expensive) visits to their dependents or tenants. A 1612 citation in the *OED* remarks that "the lord . . . did eat them out of house and home." The noun is *coshery*.

cosmothetic [kahz-moh-**thet**-ik] an adjective meaning 'something that assumes there is an external world'. It is used about a theory of perception that posits the existence of an external world but denies that we have any evidence of it or knowledge about it. Perhaps useful for describing such statements such as "I know there are people who put mayonnaise on hot dogs, but I've never met one myself." From Greek words meaning 'world' plus 'positing'.

crumenically [kroo-**mee**-nick-lee] an adverb meaning 'relating to the purse'. One of many coinages by Samuel Taylor Coleridge (1772–1834), who obviously had quite a bit of time on his hands, and often financial worries on his mind.

cryptaesthesia [krip-tiss-**thee**-zhuh] any kind of supernormal perception, including clairvoyance and telepathy. From *crypto-* and a Greek word meaning 'perception'.

cuadrilla [kwah-**drill**-yuh] the troupe belonging to a matador, including his picadors, banderilleros, and a cachetero.

cultrivorous [kul-**triv**-er-us] a rare adjective meaning 'swallowing (or pretending to swallow) knives'. From Latin words meaning 'knife' and 'to devour'.

cumber-ground [**kum**-ber-ground] a person who needlessly takes up space, especially someone who is useless in his or her job.

cunctipotent [kungk-**tip**-uh-tunt] an ill-sounding synonym for *omnipotent*, with the same meaning. *Cunctitenent* means 'having all things'.

cuniculous [kyoo-**nick**-yuh-lus] an obsolete adjective meaning 'full of rabbits'. Suitable for stereotypical magicians everywhere. From a Latin word meaning 'abounding in caves'.

curculionidous [kur-kyoo-lee-**ah**-ni-dus] an adjective meaning 'pertaining to weevils'. Now you can say, "Please don't tell me that *curculionidous* pun again!"

curwhibble [kur-**whib**-ble] a thingamajig, a whatchamacallit.

cymbocephalic [sim-boh-suh-**fal**-ick] having a skull shaped like a boat, especially when seen from above; having a long and narrow skull. From Greek words meaning 'boat' and 'head'.

dactylioglyph [dack-**till**-ee-uh-gliff] an engraver of (finger) rings or the inscription of the name of the engraver or artist on a ring or gem. *Dactyliology* is the study of finger rings, and *dactyliomancy* is the art of telling the future by means of finger rings.

dactylonomy [dack-tuh-**lah**-nuh-mee] the science of counting on your fingers. A nice saving term for people who are bad at math. "I'm a *dactylonomist*, actually. It's very difficult to be a good one." *Chisanbop* is a Korean method of using the fingers as an abacus; on the left hand each finger is counted as ten and the thumb as fifty and on the right hand the thumb is five and the fingers each one. So counting 22 would involve pressing down the first two fingers on the left hand and the first two of the right; adding the thumb of the left and the remaining two fingers of the right add 52; then you can read the total, 74, from your pressed-down fingers. *Chisanbop* comes from Korean words meaning 'finger counting method'.

darraign [der-**rain**] to prepare someone to fight, to fit someone out for battle. Also, to decide something by combat (other than who's the best fighter). This word comes from an Old French word meaning 'to explain, defend'.

deesis [dee-**ee**-sis] an invocation of, or address to, a supreme being.

dejerate [**dedj**-uh-rate] an obsolete word meaning 'to take an oath, to swear to something'.

DELASSATION ROW

delassation [dee-lass-**say**-shun] fatigue, tiredness. Even saying *delassation* makes you tired. From a Latin word meaning 'to tire out'.

deliciate [di-**lish**-ee-ate] an unfortunately obsolete word meaning 'to make yourself happy; to indulge; to revel'. Perhaps through *abligurition?*

delitescent [dell-i-**tess**-unt] an adjective meaning 'hidden, concealed'.

desticate [**des**-ti-kate] a deservedly rare and obsolete word that means 'to squeak like a rat'. Perhaps due, though, for a new life in mobster shows. The noun *destication*, 'squeaking', isn't much more common.

deturpate [**dee**-tur-pate] an ugly word with an ugly meaning: 'to disfigure, to defile'. From Latin words meaning 'to make ugly'.

deuterogamist [d(y)oo-ter-**rah**-guh-mist] someone who marries a second time. Or, as the old joke goes, an optimist.

dignotion [dig-**noh**-shun] a distinguishing mark or sign. This seems to have a mainly abstract use, instead of being a quick way to say "any birthmarks, tattoos, scars, or brandings?" From a Latin word meaning 'to distinguish'.

dilluing [dill-**loo**-ing] the process of sorting ore by washing it in a hand sieve. Also written *deluing*. It would be surprising if any of the prospectors of 1848, or any other gold rush, knew this word for their activity.

discerp [dis-**surp**] to tear something to shreds, to tear something apart, to separate. From a Latin word meaning 'pluck'.

drail [drale] an obsolete word meaning 'a long trailing headdress'. However, the vagaries of fashion being what they are, who knows if it will remain obsolete?

draisine [dray-**zeen**] the earliest kind of bicycle, named after its inventor, Baron von Drais of Sauerbrun. He called it a *swiftwalker* (he was a modest fellow, it seems). It was also called a *dandy-horse*.

Drawcansir [draw-**kan**-ser] someone who kills or injures both friend and foe. From the name of a blustering, bragging character in George Villiers's burlesque play *The Rehearsal,* who in the last scene is made to enter a battle and to kill all the combatants on both sides. His name might be intended to suggest drawing a can of liquor, as there are references to his drinking capacity in the fourth act of the play.

drazel [**drazz**-zle] a slut. Of unknown origin, perhaps connected with the Scots word *drasie,* which may or may not mean 'phlegmatic'.

dretch [drech] an obsolete word meaning both 'to trouble in sleep' and 'to be troubled in sleep'. It's from an Old English word and is unknown in other Germanic languages, although we know that everyone has bad dreams, at least occasionally. A citation from Malory's *Le Morte d'Arthur* reads "We alle … were soo dretched that somme of vs lepte oute of oure beddes naked," which must be the canonical bad awakening.

drinkdom [**dringk**-dum] the influence of the alcoholic beverage industry, or the power of drink. The *OED* gives an 1885 citation, "The triumph of *drinkdom* over temperance."

drogulus [**drah**-gyuh-lus] something the presence of which cannot be verified, usually a disembodied being, because it has no physical effects. Coined by the philosopher A. J. Ayer, possibly by association with *dragon.*

dromaeognathous [drah-mee-**agg**-nuh-thus] having a palate like than of an emu. This is such a wonderful word that it's a shame that most people would have to work extremely hard to wangle this into conversation. In fact, it may be impossible.

drong [drahng] a narrow lane or alley. From an Old English word meaning 'to press, to compress'.

drumble [**drum**-ble] to move in a slow or sluggish way, to be lazy. Also, to drone or mumble.

druxy [**druck**-see] an adjective meaning 'having rotten spots concealed by healthy wood'. A nice candidate for extension—how many rotten things are concealed by seemingly sound exteriors?

dulocracy [doo-**lah**-kruh-see] government by slaves. Used mostly in the sense of "heaven forbid these inferior people ever rule us," instead of "finally the enslaved get their turn and rightful place." This word doesn't seem have been used much even in the heated antebellum era, when you would have thought it would get a workout.

dulosis [d(y)oo-**loh**-sis] the technical term for the enslavement of ants, by ants. The adjective is *dulotic*. Sadly, there has never been an ant Abraham Lincoln, so there is no ant Emancipation Proclamation, or even any ant Harriet Beecher Stowe.

dyslogistic [dis-luh-**djiss**-tick] expressing disapproval or opprobrium. The antonym of *eulogistic*.

dysteleology [dis-tell-ee-**ah**-luh-djee] the study of the organs of plants and animals without admitting that there is any purpose to their design. The antonym is *teleology*, studying things with the idea that there is a purpose for everything in nature. Someone who is unwilling to admit the existence of design in nature has *teleophobia*.

ECHOPRAXIA

E

eadness [**ed**-niss] an obsolete word meaning 'happiness, luxury'. From an Old English word meaning 'wealth'. It seems that the idea of money buying happiness is very old in English—this word has a citation from the year 1000.

eblandish [ee-**blan**-dish] an obsolete and rare word meaning 'to get by coaxing or flattery', from a Latin word with the same meaning.

eboulement [ay-**bool**-munt] the crumbling or falling of a wall, especially a fortification. This is another good word demanding figurative use. "She's still hanging up when I call, but I'm hoping for an *eboulement* soon."

eccaleobion [eck-kal-ee-oh-**bye**-un] the name given to an egg-hatching machine invented in 1839 by a W. Bucknell. The name is supposed to be the sentence "I evoke life" written as one Greek word. It has been used figuratively; a citation from 1880 in the *OED* says that a particular magazine was "at one time a very *eccaleöbion* for young writers."

echopraxia [eck-oh-**prack**-see-uh] the meaningless imitation of the movements of others, probably including that parlor trick where you yawn or scratch your nose and watch the movement make its way through all the people in a room. From 'echo' and the Greek word for 'action'.

emmetropia [em-uh-**troh**-pee-uh] the condition of the eye in which no correction of vision is needed—in other words, 20/20 vision or better. From Greek words meaning '(well) proportioned' and 'eye'. If both eyes have the same vision, they are *isometropic.*

emulous [**em**-yuh-lus] an adjective meaning 'wanting to rival or imitate, wanting to obtain'. It also means 'motivated by rivalry' or 'greedy for praise or power'. This last meaning is a reasonable extension, for who is *emulous* of someone weak or despised? This word is a nice way to say *envious, jealous,* and *emulative,* all at once.

enchorial [en-**kor**-ee-ul] an adjective meaning 'used in or belonging to a particular country'. It comes from a Greek word meaning 'in or of the country'. An 1882 citation from the *OED* reads "That indescribable *enchorial* something which is British and not Netherlandish."

entermete [en-tur-**meet**] an obsolete word meaning 'to meddle, to concern oneself (with something)', the implication being of course "something that is none of your business." From two Latin forms, one meaning 'to interrupt', the other meaning 'to send'.

epagomenic [ep-uh-**gah**-muh-nick] denoting days left off the calendar (before calendar reform). Also, gods worshiped on those days. This would be a lovely word to use for holidays that are personal but not public; birthdays, anniversaries, mental health days, and the like. "I need next Tuesday off, it's an *epagomenic* day."

ephorize [ef-uh-rize] to rule, to have a controlling influence on. From the title given to magistrates in various Dorian states, especially Sparta, where the five *ephors*, appointed annually by popular election, exercised a controlling power over the kings. From a Greek word meaning 'overseer'.

epirot [ip-**pye**-rut] a person who lives inland, not on the coast. From a Greek word meaning 'mainland'. A word that those of us in "flyover country" can use with pride.

epithymy [i-**pith**-uh-mee] a rare word meaning 'desire, lust'. The term is obsolete, but the adjective of choice that pairs with this idea hasn't changed since 1600: the *OED* citation has "hot *epithymie*."

equivoque [**eck**-wuh-voke] something that has the same name as something else, such as the six Sarahs in your child's class at school.

etaoin shrdlu [ett-oh-in **shurd**-loo] the letters set by hitting the first two vertical banks of keys on the left side of the keyboard of a Linotype machine. This sequence is used as a temporary placeholder but is also sometimes printed by mistake. *Etaoin shrdlu* is also used to mean any error-filled sequence of type.

eustress [**yoo**-stress] good stress, such as a promotion or a new baby. It makes you happy, it makes you crazy, but with a little more happy than crazy. From Greek *eu-* ('good') and *stress*.

EXTRAORDINARY
AND EXCITING
EXCLAMATIONS

Although we can be sure that human emotions haven't changed much, if at all, during the past several millennia, the words we use to show those emotions—or to add stress or emphasis or agreement—certainly have.

Not very many people have used *adad!* since the late 1700s, no matter how strongly they feel the need to emphasize their feelings. (The last citation in the *OED* is "Why you look as fresh and bloomy to-day—Adad, you little slut, I believe you are painted" from 1763.) Likewise, *avoy!* as 'an expression of fear, surprise, or remonstrance' hasn't seen much use either. (The last citation, from 1393, being "Avoy my lorde, I am a maide.") *Coads-nigs!*, an expression of surprise, would be itself surprising to hear today.

Many a light oath of the last couple of centuries, however relieving to the feelings of those who once said them, are opaque today. *Ifegs!*, *ifads!*, *ivads!*, *mafey!*, and *fegs!*, all expressing astonishment and all related to *faith*, would be usefully resurrected by those wanting that hard-to-achieve swashbuckling air. Even more swashbuckling and devil-may-care is *jernie!*, an oath meaning 'I renounce God' (originally from the French *je renie Dieu*). *'Sdines* ('by God's *dines*', or 'dignity') lacks strength as an oath, but you have to admire the invention of *'Slidikins!* ('by God's eyelids'). Exclaiming *'Snails!* might cause people to look for slimy little shelled creatures and wonder about your phobic tendencies; nobody would think that you were swearing 'by God's nails'.

Fludgs! meaning 'quickly' is wasted in a dusty corner of the dictionary: *Fludgs!*—bring it back! *Gip!* and *gup!*, used to express irritation to a horse, don't seem to be that useful today, unless people want non-digital ways to express their impatience with other drivers. *Hissa!*, used by seamen when hauling or hoisting, doesn't translate well to the metaphorical heavy lifting many of us do during the workday. And *hyke!* or *stoo!*, used to call dogs to the chase, won't do so much for motivating the football team. *Sess!*, used to call a dog to dinner, though, could be picked up again by dogs fairly quickly. Cats may still have to listen for the can opener.

> *Tphrowh!*, used to draw attention, would be useful if only I had a clue as to how to pronounce it.

Ichane!, an expression of sorrow (possibly from a Gaelic word meaning 'oh, alas'), still sounds suitably sad and lonesome; *tilly-vally!*, meaning 'nonsense', is likewise still perfectly clear, but *lew!* meaning 'behold' is now just silly. *Proface!* as an expression of good wishes at dinner (from a French phrase meaning 'may it do you good') would be a nice way to start a meal. *Tphrowh!*, used to draw attention, would be useful if only I had a clue as to how to pronounce it. (I'm sure all my efforts at doing so would draw attention, if not the kind I was hoping for.) It's also hard to believe that *wahahowe!* ever served anybody well as an expression of surprise; it looks more like a transliteration of a sneeze. *Zoonters!*, on the other hand, could come out of the mouth of any fourteen-year-old on the planet: *"Zoonters* they're gone" is the citation in the *OED*. Well, *zoonters!* These words may be gone for now, but it doesn't mean they can't come back.

fiant [**fee**-unt] an obsolete word, used especially of badgers and foxes, meaning 'to cast excrement'.

finifugal [fye-**nif**-yoo-gul] an adjective meaning 'shunning the end (of anything)'. Appropriate both for children avoiding bedtime and for those folks who "just don't want the book to end."

finnesko [**finz**-koh] a boot made of reindeer skin tanned with birch, with the hair left on the outside. A fashion statement made on early polar expeditions and trips across Greenland.

finnimbrun [fin-**nim**-brun] a knickknack, a trinket.

fiscelle [fis-**sell**] a little basket. Probably one of those baskets which somehow seem to persist, filled with paper clips and unrecognizable parts of unremembered objects, long after the original contents have vanished.

fistiana [fis-tee-**ann**-uh] a humorous word meaning 'of or relating to the fists or boxing'. Synonyms are *fistic* and *fistical*; the *OED* haughtily remarks that these words 'are not in dignified use'.

fittyland [**fit**-ee-land] the near horse of the rearmost pair hitched to a plow, which walks on the unplowed part while the far horse walks in the furrow.

FLAFFER

flaffer [**flaff**-er] to rustle when moving, to flutter. The citations in the *OED* seem to show that this word was used mostly about birds, but it seems like a useful word for impractical dresses.

flambuginous [flam-**byoo**-djuh-nus] a rare adjective meaning 'deceptive, fictitious, sham'. Related to the *flam* of *flimflam* and *flamfew*, 'a gewgaw'. *Flamfew* is related to a Latin word meaning 'a bubble, a lie'.

Flamingantism [flam-ing-**gah**-tiz-um] the policy of encouraging and furthering the use of Flemish. The implied context is "in Belgium" but it would be funnier to see *Flamingantism* everywhere.

flaskisable [**flas**-kuh-suh-ble] an obsolete adjective meaning 'changeable'. From an Old French word meaning 'to bend'. Used mostly about people, this is a nice substitute for 'flaky'.

fleechment [**fleech**-munt] flattery, cajolery, persuasive but untruthful talk. Its origin is obscure.

flemensfirth [**flem**-unz-firth] an Old English law term for the crime of harboring a banished person. It's a corruption of an Old English term that literally means 'entertainment of fugitives', which makes you wonder that if the fugitives aren't having a really good time, is it still a crime? What if they're only smiling politely?

flosculous [**flahs**-kyuh-lus] an adjective meaning 'like a flower' or 'flowery'. From a Latin word meaning 'little flower', which also gives us *floscule*, 'something shaped like a little flower' or 'a flowery speech' and *flosculation*, 'speaking in a flowery way'.

frigoric [fri-**gor**-ik] an imagined, nonexistent substance supposed to be the cause of cold. It's a charming idea; as if, during winter, you could just slap on some *frigoric*-repellent like sunscreen and go out happily in your bathing suit.

furciferous [fur-**sif**-er-us] an adjective meaning 'like a rascal'. From a Latin word meaning 'fork-bearer', which, by analogy with the forked yoke put on the necks of criminals, also came to mean 'jailbird'.

G

galimatias [gal-uh-**mat**-ee-us] nonsense, meaningless talk. Of unknown origin, first found in the sixteenth century.

gangrel [**gang**-grul] a child just beginning to walk.

geason [**ghee**-zun] an adjective meaning 'rare, uncommon', and thus also 'extraordinary, amazing'. Some of the words in this book should embody both meanings of *geason*, if we've done things right.

genizah [guh-**nee**-zuh] a repository for damaged, discarded, or heretical books. From a Hebrew word meaning 'set aside, hide'.

genyplasty [**jen**-i-plas-tee] the name for reconstructive surgery of the cheek when it has been disfigured or is congenitally defective. From Greek words meaning 'cheek' and 'molded'. Since so many body parts have figurative meanings (*hand, backbone, stomach*) this could be used with the figurative meaning of *cheek*—giving someone the ability to answer back saucily when they have either lost it or never had it in the first place.

geoponic [djee-uh-**pah**-nick] an adjective meaning 'relating to farming or agriculture', and, like most farming words, it has an extended humorous meaning of 'rustic, countrified'. As a noun, *geoponic* means 'a book about agriculture' or 'a writer on agricultural topics'. A *geoponist* is a student of agriculture.

gilly-gaupus [gil-ee-**gaw**-pus] an awkward or foolish person. A *gaw-pus* is also a silly person. Other words for a silly person include *chrisom* and *dotterel*.

glaikery [**glay**-kuh-ree] foolish or giddy conduct. *Glaik* is defined in the *OED* as 'mocking deception'.

gleed [gleed] a live coal, or a beam of light. This word was used in a few equally obsolete similes, such as *as red* (or *hot* or *fierce*) *as a gleed* and *to burn* (or *glow* or *glister* or *glitter*) *as a gleed*.

gleimous [**glay**-mus] a rare word meaning 'full of phlegm or mucus'. If only the condition of being full of phlegm was as rare as this word for it. *Gleimousness* is stickiness, but if something is *engleimous* it is both slimy and venomous (a winning combination). The etymology of *gleim* itself is thankfully obscure.

gloze [glohz] a note in the margin, or a commentary or explanation in a text. This word is related to *gloss* and *glossary*, and comes from a Greek word meaning 'tongue'. To *make gloze* is a rare verb phrase meaning 'to talk smoothly or flatteringly to'.

gnap [nap] an obsolete word meaning 'to bite in a snapping way'; also, 'to criticize', or 'to clip words when speaking'. Of onomatopoeic origin.

gnast [nast] an obsolete word meaning 'a spark; the snuff of a candle'.

halewey [**hal**-uh-way] an obsolete word for a kind a healing water used both internally and as a lotion. Obviously before the coining of the phrase 'for external use only'. One suspects that *halewey* was alcoholic in nature to serve such a dual purpose.

halieutic [hal-i-**yoo**-tik] an adjective meaning 'of or about fishing'. Ultimately from a Greek word meaning 'the sea'.

harbergery [**har**-ber-djuh-ree] a place of entertainment, an inn. From an Old French word meaning 'to lodge'. Grab it as the name for your restaurant now.

haslet [**hay**-slit] a piece of meat for roasting, especially the entrails of a pig or the heart or liver of a sheep or calf. From an Old French word meaning 'roasted meat'. *Hastery* is the art of roasting meat, or a collective term for roast meats. (Yet another good restaurant name.)

hastilude [**hass**-tle-ude] a kind of tournament involving spears. From Latin words meaning 'spear' and 'play'.

haucepy [**hoh**-suh-pee] a kind of trap for wild animals, especially wolves. From a French word meaning 'to lift up the foot'.

hautain [haw-**tane**] an obsolete adjective meaning 'proud, arrogant', or (of the voice) 'raised, loud'. From an Old French word meaning 'high'.

heinsby [**haynz**-bee] an obsolete word defined in the *OED* as 'a mean wretch'. Possibly related to the verb *hain*, 'to keep from spending or consuming'.

heptamerous [hep-**tam**-er-us] an adjective meaning 'having seven parts or members'.

heterarchy [**het**-er-ahr-kee] government by strangers or foreigners. Literally, 'rule of an alien', which leaves itself open to so *many* jokes that I can't pick just one.

heterography [het-uh-**rah**-gruh-fee] an obsolete and rare word meaning 'incorrect spelling'. Also, *inorthography*. How much better to say, "I'm an *inorthographist*" than to admit you can't spell worth a damn?

hibernacle [**hye**-ber-nack-kle] a winter retreat, or the winter home of a hibernating animal. From a Latin word meaning 'wintry'. "I have a little *hibernacle* in Florida" is a lovely sentence from October through April.

hiccius doccius [**hick**-shee-us **dock**-she-us] a word like 'abracadabra' or 'presto', used by jugglers when performing tricks. By extension, a word for a juggler or someone who cuts corners. This may be a corruption of the Latin phrase *hicce est doctus* 'this is the learned man', or perhaps just a nonsense phrase that sounds like Latin.

hoddypeak [**hah**-dee-peek] an obsolete word meaning 'a fool or blockhead'.

hodograph [**hah**-doh-graff] a machine for registering the paces of a horse (to better tell one from another). From Greek words meaning 'way' and 'writing'.

hofles [**hofe**-liss] an obsolete word meaning 'excessive, unreasonable'. From an Old Norse word meaning 'immoderate'.

holagogue [**hah**-loh-gog] a medicine that is supposed to get rid of all 'morbid humours'. (A lovely name for an antidepressant, if Big Pharma is listening.)

hookum-snivey [**hook**-um-**sniv**-ee] any fakery or deceit. Also, any contraption used for unlocking a door from the outside (other than a key, of course).

huderon [**hyoo**-der-un] an obsolete adjective meaning 'lazy'. The singsongy citation from 1721 reads "a morning-sleep is worth a foldful of sheep to a huderon duderon Daw'. A *daw* is a sluggard; *duderon* is undefined and probably just reduplicative, as in *higgledy-piggledy*.

iatraliptic [eye-at-ruh-**lip**-tick] a doctor who cures diseases with lotions or creams. As an adjective it means 'of or about the curing of diseases with lotions or creams'.

ichneutic [ick-**n(y)oo**-tick] an adjective meaning 'relating to trackers or tracking'.

ichnography [ick-**nog**-ruh-fee] a floor plan for a building. From Greek words meaning 'track' and 'writing'.

ichnomancy [ick-**noh**-mun-see] the science of making deductions about people and animals by examining their footsteps. The *OED* citation from 1855 seems to imply that you may find out "figure, peculiarities, occupations, &c, of men or beasts" by this method. From Greek words meaning 'track' and 'divination'.

ichoglan [**itch**-oh-glan] a page waiting in the palace of the Sultan. From Turkish words that mean 'interior' and 'young man'. In this definition, 'waiting' obviously means 'serving', but it's so much more poetic to understand it as 'to stay in expectation of'. What is he waiting *for*? Alas, the Sultan has fled, and we will never know.

iconomicar [eye-kuh-**nah**-mi-ker] a writer about agriculture. A synonym (surprising that we need one) for *geoponic*.

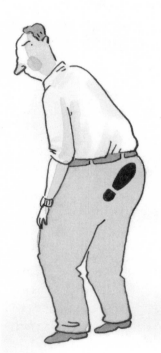

ICHNEUTIC

icterical [ick-**terr**-i-kle] an adjective meaning 'tinged with yellow'. *Luteolous* is another adjective meaning 'yellowish'. *Flavescate* is a rare, obsolete adjective that means 'to make yellow'.

ideokinetic [eye-dee-oh-ki-**net**-ik] a kind of apraxia in which the sufferer still has the physical ability to perform an action or movement and understands a request to perform it, but is unable to do so when asked. This might be a good technical name for the common phenomenom of being able to perform astounding physical or mental feats, but not if anyone is watching.

idioticon [id-ee-**oh**-ti-kun] a dictionary of words used in one region only.

ignoscency [ig-**noh**-sun-see] a rare and obsolete word meaning 'forgiveness'. From a Latin word meaning 'to take no notice of'.

ignotism [**ig**-nuh-tiz-um] an obsolete word meaning 'a mistake due to ignorance'.

illecebrous [ill-**less**-uh-brus] an obsolete word meaning 'attractive, alluring'. From a Latin word meaning 'to entice'.

ilspile [**ill**-spill] a hedgehog. There are a surprising number of names for the hedgehog: *cirogrille* (actually a hyrax, but understood by medieval writers to be a hedgehog), *echinus* (Latin for hedgehog, but used as an English word by some early writers), *furze-pig, herisson, hotchi witchu* (the Romany name for the hedgehog), *hurcheon, irchepil, irspile, il* (or *ile*), *irchon* (or *irchin*), *tiggy,* and *urchin.*

imberb [im-**burb**] a rare adjective meaning 'beardless'. *Imberbic* is another form. It comes from *im-* plus the Latin *barba*, 'beard'.

imbost [im-**boast**] the foam in 'foaming at the mouth'. The *OED* has it as 'foam from the mouth of a beast'. As a verb, it means to harass someone or something until they foam at the mouth, or to drive someone to madness.

imbriferous [im-**brif**-er-us] bringing rain; rainy. From a Latin word meaning 'a shower'.

immerd [im-**murd**] a rare word meaning 'to cover something in dung or ordure'. From a Latin word meaning 'dung'.

immram [**im**-ram] a kind of Irish sea story in which the hero, along with a few boon companions, wanders from island to island having wonderful adventures. The best known recount the adventures of St. Brendan, who is also occasionally credited with having discovered America in his last voyage.

impaludism [im-**pal**-yoo-diz-um] a diseased state, including enlargement of the spleen and frequent fevers, found in marsh dwellers. This is probably what we now call malaria (which comes from Italian 'bad air'). This word comes from the Latin for 'marsh'.

imparidigitate [im-parr-i-**didj**-i-tate] having an odd number of digits (toes or fingers) on each limb. The specific word for having an odd number of toes is *perissodactyl*. *Imparidigitate* comes from Latin for 'unequal' plus 'digit'; *perissodactyl* comes from the Greek for 'uneven' plus 'digit'.

impeticos [im-**pet**-i-kahs] a word written in dialogue to make the speaker seem foolish. From Shakespeare's *Twelfth Night*, act 2, scene 3, said by Feste. Apparently it is a form of *impocket*, 'put in one's pocket', and was perhaps intended to suggest *petticoat*.

> *Sir Andrew:* I sent thee sixe pence for thy Lemon, hadst it?
> *Feste:* I did impeticos thy gratillity.

impigrous [im-**pig**-grus] an obsolete and rare adjective meaning 'quick, diligent'. *Impigrity* is the noun; both come from *im-* and the Latin word *piger*, 'sluggish'.

impluvious [im-**ploo**-vee-us] a rare adjective meaning 'wet with rain'.

inaniloquent [in-an-**nill**-uh-kwunt] an obsolete and rare adjective meaning 'full of idle talk, foolishly babbling'. From Latin words meaning 'inane' and 'to speak'. Other forms include *inaniloquous, inaniloquence,* and *inaniloquation.*

incompt [in-**kahmpt**] an obsolete adjective meaning 'messy, inelegant'. From a Latin word meaning 'unadorned, rough'.

incontunded [in-kun-**tun**-did] an obsolete adjective meaning 'not bruised or pounded'. One would hope this would be an adjective applicable to all people, everywhere, all the time. It seems to be used mostly about spices and fruit.

infelicific [in-fee-luh-**sif**-ik] an adjective meaning 'making unhappy'. This is mostly used in the discussion of ethics, with citations like "The breach of any moral rule is pro tanto *infelicific* from its injurious effects on moral habits generally."

INTRIGUING AND INCREDIBLE -IST WORDS

The handy suffix -ist has found its way onto many a weird and wonderful word. Of course, if you are an *acosmist*, you deny the existence of the universe, which also lets out any belief in the suffix -ist.

If you're an *adiabolist*, you don't believe in the existence of a devil, although it's possible to at the same time be a *diablerist*, someone who paints or draws pictures in which devils appear. A *demonurgist* is someone who practices magic with the help of demons (it's much easier, I guess, with a few extra hands to hold things, and to fill out the chanting). An *energumenist* is one possessed by a demon, or someone who is a fanatical enthusiast for something.

A *battologist* has nothing to do with bats, in the ordinary way of things—instead he or she needlessly repeats the same thing, needlessly, needlessly. *Biloquists* can speak in two different voices (if they are also *gastriloquists*, one of those voices will seem to come from their bellies). A *heterophemist* is someone who says something other than what he or she meant to say. (I hope never to meet a heterophemic biloquistical gastriloquist.) A *neoterist* is someone who favors new words and expressions. A *phlyarologist* is someone who 'talks nonsense'. A *querulist* is someone who complains (*a lot* is implied).

We would all like to feel that we are *antisocordists*, opponents of sloth or stupidity, although it's more likely that we are *inadvertists*, people who 'habitually fail to take notice', or are consistently oblivious. A *crinanthropist* is someone who 'judges mankind' (and most likely finds it wanting). A *malist* is someone who believes that this world, though not the worst possible world, is still pretty bad. A *psychrolutist* is someone who recommends cold baths, and a *carcerist* is someone who advocates prisons, although it's likely there's a lot of overlap between those two groups.

A *cereologist* is someone who investigates crop circles (at significant risk of alien abduction). A *fumifugist* is someone who drives away smoke (or, perhaps, someone who drives away smokers). A *heartist* is a fencer who can pierce the heart (with an actual sword, not with words or melting glances). A *bouquinist* is a dealer in secondhand books of little value. A *pyrgologist* is someone who is an expert in the history and structure of towers. A *tziganologist* studies Hungarian gypsies.

> I hope never to meet a heterophemic biloquistical gastriloquist.

An *Exarchist* is someone who supports the Exarch of Bulgaria against the Patriarch of Constantinople, come what may. An *elaterist* is someone who explains certain phenomena as being due to the elasticity of the air. (Good enough for me.) A *gymnobiblist* is someone who believes that the unannotated text of the Bible is enough of a guide to religious truth for even the least-educated person. A *juredivinist* is a believer in the divine right of kings. A *chorizontist* is someone who believes (most likely with fanatical enthusiasm) that the *Iliad* and the *Odyssey* were the fruits of different authors, and thus is more than likely someone you do not want to be seated next to at dinner.

A *nuxodeltiologist* is someone who collects postcards that show nighttime scenes. An *exonumist* is someone who collects things that look like coins, but aren't. I haven't found a word for someone who collects -*ist* words; coinages gratefully accepted care of the publisher.

inficete [in-fuh-**seet**] a rare adjective meaning 'unfacetious, not witty'. One of the citations from the *OED*, from Thomas Love Peacock's novel of *Crotchet Castle* (1831), is this lovely exchange:

> *Mr. E.:* Sir, you are very facetious at my expense.
>
> *Dr. F.:* Sir, you have been very unfacetious, very inficete at mine.

influous [**in**-floo-us] an obsolete and rare adjective meaning 'shedding astral influence'. In other words, what you do when your horoscope for the day is bad and you resolve to take no notice of it.

infrendiate [in-**fren**-dee-ate] to gnash the teeth. It almost makes you *infrendiate* just to say it.

infucate [**in**-fyoo-kate] to use makeup. Earlier definitions were 'to paint the face, to color the face artificially'. The word sounds as impious and obscene as the practice was thought to be! The noun is even worse: *infucation*.

inhebetate [in-**heb**-i-tate] to make something dull or blunt. Everyone knows a person who can *inhebetate* the most exciting story. Unfortunately.

isangelous [eye-**san**-djuh-lus] an obsolete and rare adjective meaning 'equal to the angels'. The citation from the *OED* is "Let us look back upon ourselves, who we expect shall one day be made *isangelous*, equal to the angels."

isocephaly [eye-soh-**sef**-uh-lee] the principle observed in some ancient Greek reliefs, especially in friezes, of representing the heads of all the figures at nearly the same level. (This is often now done in movies or at press conferences to give the illusion of all the participants being the same height.)

isocracy [eye-**sah**-kruh-see] a system of government in which all the people possess equal political power. The citation in the *OED* from 1652 shows that we have always been cynical about the practicality of this idea: "It remaineth doubtfull, whether people who live together, may lawfully retain an *Isocracie* among them." An *isocrat* is an advocate of *isocracy*; to *isocratize* is to practice *isocracy*. The equality of people before the law, or the equality of political rights among the citizens of a state, is *isonomy*.

iteroparous [it-er-**rah**-per-us] an adjective used to describe organisms that have multiple sets of offspring, or that give birth more than once during the organism's life cycle. An organism that reproduces only once during its life is *semelparous*, a plant that fruits only once and dies is *monocarpic*. The *iter*- here is the same *iter*- as in *iteration; semel*- comes from a Latin word meaning 'once'.

ithand [**eye**-thund] an obsolete Scottish word meaning 'diligent, busy', or 'uninterrupted'. Which makes this word its own antonym, because busy people are constantly interrupted, usually by someone who stands in the doorway saying "I know you're busy, but . . . ."

jactance [**jack**-tunce] a rare word meaning 'boasting'.

jaculiferous [jack-yuh-**lif**-er-us] an adjective meaning 'having prickles'. Could certainly be used to replace the overworn "He's got a chip on his shoulder the size of Texas!"

jannock [**jan**-uk] a dialect adjective meaning 'fair, genuine'. It's one of those words used frequently in the negative, as in "that's not *jannock!*" Also used as an adverb: "Act *jannock*, or else I'll turn this car around, I swear!"

jargogle [**jar**-goh-gle] an obsolete verb meaning 'to confuse, to mix up'. The probable adjective, *jargogled*, sounds almost onomatopoeic.

jau dewin [**jaw** duh-win] a term of reproach, of obscure origin, from the late 1300s. No matter what the origin, we can always use another term of reproach.

javanais [zhah-vah-**nay**] a French slang, like pig Latin, in which *av* or *va* is introduced after each syllable or word.

jectigation [jeck-ti-**gay**-shun] a wagging or trembling movement. From a Latin word meaning 'to throw'.

jentation [jen-**tay**-shun] a rare and obsolete word meaning 'breakfast'. Also, *jenticulation. Jenticulate* is the verb, meaning 'to breakfast'.

jettatura [jet-uh-**toor**-uh] the evil eye, bad luck. From an Italian word meaning 'person who brings bad luck'. A citation in the *OED* from the *Glasgow Herald* of 1921 says, "This simple remedy is much in use throughout Italy to-day as an antidote to the evil power of the *Jettatore*." Annoyingly, and dangerously, the remedy is not named.

jirble [**jur**-ble] to spill liquid by unsteady movement of the container; to pour liquid from vessel to vessel. Of onomatopoeic origin.

JOLLOPING JOLLUX

jocoserious [joh-koh-**sear**-ee-us] half jocular, half serious; partly silly and partly somber; blending jokes and serious matters. The noun, used only once, is *jocoseriosity*.

joinpee [**join**-pee] an obsolete and rare adjective meaning 'with the feet joined or put close together'.

jollop [**joll**-lup] to make a noise like a turkey. As a noun it means 'the cry of a turkey'. Unfortunately, it doesn't seem to have been used in any Thanksgiving poetry.

jollux [**joll**-luks] an obsolete slang term meaning 'a fat person'.

kakistocracy [kack-i-**stah**-kruh-see] the government of a state by its worst citizens. The adjective is *kakistocratical*. A lovely piece of rhetoric is the 1876 citation in the *OED:*

> Is ours a government of the people, by the people, for the people, or a Kakistocracy rather, for the benefit of knaves at the cost of fools?

kalokagathia [kal-oh-kuh-**gath**-ee-uh] nobility and goodness of character. From Greek words meaning 'beautiful' and 'good', describing the perfect character.

kamagraphy [kuh-**mag**-gruh-fee] the process of making copies of paintings, using a special press and treated canvas, which reproduces exactly the color and texture of the original brushstrokes. However, the citations seem to suggest that it destroys the original painting in the process, so it's not exactly what the counterfeiters and forgers of the world have been waiting for.

karmadharaya [kahr-muh-**dahr**-ee-uh] a compound word in which the first part of the word describes the second, such as *highway* (adjective + noun) or *steamboat* (attributive noun + noun). From a Sanskrit word meaning 'holding, bearing'.

katavothron [kat-uh-**vah**-thrun] a subterranean channel or deep chasm formed by running water. From Greek words meaning 'swallow' and 'hole'.

kathenotheism [kath-**en**-oh-thee-iz-um] a kind of polytheism where each god is single and supreme in turn. From a Greek word meaning 'one by one' and -*theism*.

kench [kentch] an obsolete and rare word meaning 'to laugh loudly'.

kenodoxy [**kee**-nuh-dock-see] an obsolete and rare word meaning 'the love or study of boasting or vainglory'.

kishen [**kish**-un] a measure used on the Isle of Man, containing eight quarts. In the *OED*, the measured commodities are oats and potatoes; ale and coal also comes in kishens. A kishen of potatoes, it is said, should weigh twenty-one pounds, a kishen of coal slightly more.

knabble [**nab**-ul] an obsolete word meaning 'to bite or nibble'. A Google check of this word turns it up on a list that calls itself "The finest and longest collection of hamster names in the WWW!", which seems appropriate.

knackatory [**nack**-uh-tor-ee] an obsolete and rare word meaning 'a place to buy knick-knacks'. (It sounds more like a place of punishment for those who bestow too many knick-knacks upon others. "That's the third vase this year! Off to the knackatory with you!")

knaifatic [nay-uh-**fat**-ick] an adjective meaning 'knavish' or 'low-born'. In the *OED* it is labeled as obsolete, Scottish, and a nonce-word, which is surprising as you would think that the opportunities to call someone *knaifatic* would be plentiful in sixteenth-century Scotland.

kye [kie] a miserly sailor. Of unknown origin, but possibly related to a dialect word, *kyish*, meaning 'dirty'.

kyriolexy [**kye**-ree-oh-leck-see] the use of literal expressions. From Greek words meaning 'proper' and 'speaking'.

laetificant [lit-**tiff**-i-kunt] a rare adjective meaning 'antidepressant, cheering'. Usually used about medicine.

lambdacism [**lam**-duh-siz-um] too frequent use of the letter *l* in speaking or writing. Also, pronouncing the letter *r* as the letter *l* (also called *lallation*).

leathwake [**leeth**-wake] an obsolete word meaning 'having flexible joints, lithe'. From Old English words meaning 'limb' and 'soft'.

leggiadrous [ledj-ee-**add**-rus] an obsolete and rare adjective meaning 'graceful, elegant'. From an Italian word meaning 'sprightly'.

lethiferous [li-**thif**-er-us] causing death, deadly. From Latin words meaning 'death' and 'bring'.

libant [**lye**-bant] an adjective meaning 'tasting, lightly touching'. This word is related to *libation*; they both come from a Latin word meaning 'to taste'.

limbeck [**lim**-beck] to wear yourself out in the effort to have a new idea. This word ultimately comes from an Arabic word meaning 'a still', the analogy being that you distill ideas with your brain.

limitanean [lim-i-**tay**-nee-un] an adjective meaning 'on the border'. A term from Roman antiquity, it usually refers to soldiers stationed on the border. Another similar word is *limitrophe*, an adjective meaning 'on the frontier'.

linguipotence [ling-**gwip**-uh-tunce] mastery of languages or the tongue. A nonce word used once by Samuel Taylor Coleridge: "The New Testament contains not the least proof of the *linguipotence* of the Apostles, but the clearest proof of the contrary."

logion [**log**-ee-on] a traditional saying or proverb of a sage. Chiefly used with reference to the sayings of Jesus contained in the collections supposed to have been among the sources of the Gospels, or to sayings attributed to Jesus but not recorded in the Gospels. From a Greek word meaning 'oracle'.

logomachy [luh-**gah**-muh-kee] fighting about words, a fight about words. From Greek words meaning 'word' and 'fighting'. This kind of fight is always all heat and no light.

loranthaceous [lor-un-**thay**-shus] a botanical adjective that means 'related to the mistletoe family'. This word fills a gap to describe kisses given (or received) in unusual circumstances, such as under the mistletoe.

lopeholt [**lope**-hohlt] an obsolete word meaning 'a refuge, a place of safety'. Possibly from Dutch words meaning 'run' and 'hollow'.

lordswike [**lord**-swick-uh] a person who deceives their lord, a traitor. From Old English words meaning 'lord' and 'deceiver'.

loutrophoros [loo-troh-**for**-ahs] a tall vessel with two handles, used in ancient Greece to carry water to the nuptial bath. They were also put on the tombs of unmarried people. From Greek words meaning 'water for a bath' and 'carrying'.

lucifugous [loo-**sif**-yuh-gus] an adjective meaning 'shunning the light'. From Latin words meaning 'light' and 'to flee'. This was usually used as a near synonym for 'nocturnal' but seems much more poetic; instead of seeking the night, they are shunning the light. A similar adjective is *lucifugal*.

luculence [**loo**-kyoo-lunce] an obsolete and rare adjective meaning 'fineness, beauty', or 'clearness, certainty'. From a Latin word meaning 'light'.

ludibrious [loo-**dib**-ree-us] an obsolete adjective meaning 'likely to be the butt of a joke'. It can also mean 'scornful, scoffing'. It seems that one word covers all necessities: first you are made the object of mockery, and then you cover your hurt by scorning the mockers. From a Latin word meaning 'to play'.

lychnoscope [**lick**-nuh-scope] a name given to a small window, lower than the other windows, that is found in some old churches. Supposedly, the window was placed low so that the lepers outside could see the altar lights (lepers were obviously not allowed in the church itself). From Greek words meaning 'lamp' and 'look at'.

lycophosed [**lye**-kuh-fozed] an obsolete adjective meaning 'having keen sight'. From a Greek word meaning 'twilight', from roots meaning 'wolf' and 'light', which was misunderstood as 'having keen sight, like a wolf'.

macellarious [mass-uh-**lair**-ee-us] an obsolete adjective meaning 'like a butcher's' or 'like a slaughterhouse or shambles'. From a Latin word meaning 'meat market'. Perhaps the word could be renewed etymologically and be used to describe any place that exists only to encourage people to find romantic partners.

machicolation [muh-chick-uh-**lay**-shun] the opening in a wall through which fire, molten lead, stones, etc., are dropped on besiegers or attackers. Also used to mean the action of putting such things out of a machicolation.

macroseism [**mack**-roh-sye-zum] a major earthquake, or any earthquake that can be felt. Not in common use, because of the existence of the handy term 'earthquake'. *Seism* is another word that means 'earthquake'. *Macroseismic* is an adjective used to describe those effects of an earthquake that can be detected without instruments (such as buildings collapsing, pictures falling off walls, etc.) From a Greek word meaning 'to shake'. Words not derived from Greek that mean 'earthquake' include *earth-din, earth-grine* or *earth-grith, earthquave,* and *terremote.*

macrosmatic [mack-rahz-**mat**-ik] an adjective meaning 'having well-developed olfactory organs'. Also used figuratively, as in this citation from the *OED* (where the subject is George Orwell): "[he is] a *macrosmatic* writer tracking down the stench of hypocrisy or the gangrene of intellectual treachery." From *macro-* plus a Greek word meaning 'smell'.

magirology [madj-uh-**rah**-luh-djee] a rare word meaning 'the art or science of cooking'. A *magirist* (or *magirologist*) is an expert cook; something that is *magiristic* is related to cooking or cookery, and someone that is *magirological* is skilled in cooking. From a Greek word meaning 'cook'.

magnolious [mag-**noh**-lee-us] a slang word meaning 'great, splendid, magnificent, large'.

magnoperate [mag-**nah**-puh-rate] to work on one's magnum opus. Used in a letter by Lord Byron: "That is right, keep to your magnum opus—*magnoperate* away."

mesonoxian [mezz-uh-**nock**-see-un] of or related to midnight. "What are your *mesonoxian* plans?" sounds so much better on December 31 than "Hey, whatcha doin' tonight?"

moirologist [moy-**rah**-luh-jist] in Greece, a hired mourner. From Greek words meaning 'death' or 'fate' and 'speaker'. The moirologists may sing *myriologues*, extemporaneous funeral songs usually sung by women.

molendinarious [muh-len-duh-**nair**-ee-us] an obsolete adjective meaning 'of or pertaining to a mill'. *Molinology* is the study of mills and milling, which is of course done by *molinologists*, who pursue their *molinological* ends. *Molinary* means 'of or pertaining to the grinding of grain', and someone who pays to have something ground at a mill is a *multurer*.

moliminous [moh-**lim**-uh-nus] an obsolete adjective meaning 'taking great effort, laborious'. Also, 'massive, momentous'. From a Latin word meaning 'effort'.

MIGHTY AND MARVELOUS MONEY

The love of money may be the root of all evil, but it's also the root of some very interesting weird and wonderful words. There are quite a few words for people who love money, especially those who lend it to others: *danists* and *fenerators* are usurers, *mahujuns*, *soucars*, *nummularians*, and *ockerers* are moneylenders, and *collybists* are both, and misers as well. A *wisseler* is a moneychanger, and *wissel* is change for an amount of money. Lending money at usury is *gombeenism*.

Lending at interest (or *fenory*) is not the only way to make money with money. You can also literally *make* money by indulging in *fausonry* (forgery). *Shoful* is counterfeit money. To *shroff* is to separate genuine coins from counterfeit, and *shroffage* is the commission charged for doing so. If you have some good coins lying around you can shave off a bit of the valuable metal here and there, resulting in *abatude*, clipped money. It's probably easier to shave off some of the *adminicles*, the decorations that surround the main figure on a coin. If you just want to melt the whole batch down and separate the silver from the alloy, you can practice *dealbation*.

Stealing money also has a wide vocabulary. A *defalcation* is an amount of money misappropriated by someone who is in charge of it, maybe by using the *salami technique*, in which small amounts of money are transferred from many customer accounts into another account held under a false name. And there's always *chevisance*, raising money by pawning something (also, any [bad] method of raising money), or *chantage*, blackmail. A sophisticated kind of blackmail is that of the Japanese *sokaiya*, who holds a small number of shares of stock in a number of companies and attempts to extort money from them by threatening to cause trouble at the general meeting of the stockholders. Perhaps the truly desperate can go on the *kinchin-lay*, and take money from children sent on errands.

Earning money by the sweat of your brow, while not an appealing option to everyone, has its proponents. Earning by the sweat of other people's brows has many more. If you're a bishop, you can sit back and receive your *senage*, or tribute, at Easter. Technically, this doesn't make the bishop a *gyesite*, someone who accepts money in return for spiritual things (considered as a sin). A lord of the

> **Perhaps the truly desperate can go on the *kinchin-lay*, and take money from children sent on errands.**

manor can count on the annual *chevage* from each of his villeins. If you are the younger child of a king or prince, your father will have of course arranged for a suitable *appanage* to support you. Less elevated persons also had their incomes. British officers in India could at one time count on their *batta*, or extra pay for serving there, and the Lord Mayor's butler and yeoman of the cellar could look forward to their *cellarage*, money collected from the attendees at a Lord Mayor's feast.

Unfortunately, these suggestions for increasing your wealth are probably not very valuable. If they leave you with *nuppence* ('no money'), you could say that they are not worth a *rig-marie*, a *scuddick*, a *sharpshin*, a *skilligalee*, or a (brass) *razoo*—all words meaning 'a coin of very little value' and equivalent to that equally worthless *red cent*.

momurdotes [**moh**-mer-dotes] an obsolete word meaning 'the sulks'. The first part of this word may be imitative of mumbling or murmuring; the second part comes from *dote*, meaning 'to be silly, to act stupidly'.

morate [**moh**-rate] an obsolete adjective meaning 'well mannered, moral, respectable'.

morfound [**mor**-fownd] (of horses and other animals) to be chilled, to be numb with cold. From French roots meaning 'mucus' and 'melt'.

morigerate [muh-**ridj**-er-it] a rare adjective meaning 'obedient'. The noun is *morigeration*, which had the extended meaning of 'obsequiousness'. The fine shading of how and when obedience becomes obsequiousness we leave to those experts in discerning it: teachers of adolescents.

morioplasty [**mor**-ee-oh-plas-tee] the restoration of lost parts of the body. Obviously, this word is used in a surgical context, but the mental picture of two policemen at the door, asking, "Sir, is this your leg?" is a pleasant one.

morology [muh-**rah**-luh-djee] foolish talking, also, humorously, the study of fools. From a Greek word of the same meaning. A related word is *moromancy*, glossed as 'foolish divination', but more useful as a word to mean 'telling the future by observing the behavior of fools'.

motatorious [moh-tuh-**tor**-ee-us] in constant motion. Usually used about the legs of insects, a revolting concept.

muculency [**myoo**-kyuh-lun-see] an obsolete word meaning 'snottiness'.

mulciberian [mull-suh-**beer**-ee-un] an adjective meaning 'resembling Vulcan'. Originally meaning the mythological figure, but ripe to be picked up by fervent Trekkers.

multatitious [mull-tuh-**tish**-us] a rare word meaning 'acquired by fine or forfeit'. In certain localities the local police can confiscate cars and other property used in the commission of a crime; this word might be useful to them.

murenger [**myoor**-in-djer] an obsolete word meaning 'an officer who is responsible for keeping the walls of a city in good condition'.

murgeon [**mur**-djun] a plural noun meaning 'grimaces'. Its origin is obscure.

musophobist [myoo-**zah**-fuh-bist] a person who regards poetry with suspicious dislike. From Greek words meaning 'muse' and 'fear'. This word was used (and probably coined) by the poet Algernon Charles Swinburne (1837–1909), who quite possibly inspired more than a few *musophobes*.

mutuatitial [myoo-choo-uh-**tish**-ul] an obsolete and rare adjective meaning 'borrowed'. As a noun it means 'something borrowed'. The verb form is *mutuate*. They come from a Latin word meaning 'borrow'.

mycterism [**mick**-tuh-riz-um] a rare word meaning 'a taunt or sneer', from a Greek root meaning 'nose' (that being what you sneer with).

MYOMANCY

myomancy [mye-uh-man-see] divination by the movements of mice. Modern scientists probably study the movements of mice as much or more as the ancient *myomancers* ever did, and for ends that are not dissimilar.

nabocklish [na-**bock**-lish] an incredibly useful Irish interjection meaning 'Never mind! Leave that alone!' Literally meaning 'don't meddle with it'.

nacket [**nack**-it] a rude and impertinent boy. From French words meaning 'the tennis court keeper's boy'. Another *nacket*, of obscure origin, means 'a light lunch, a snack'. The two words should be easy to keep straight, unless you're a cannibal, in which case there is a pleasant congruence.

naevose [**nee**-vose] a rare adjective meaning 'spotted, freckled'. A *naevus* is a raised red or purple birthmark caused by hypertrophied blood vessels in the skin. The US spelling is *nevus*.

nanism [**nay**-niz-um] the condition of being dwarfed, or the tendency to become stunted or dwarfed. Usually used about animals and plants. *Nanity* is the condition of having any abnormal deficiency. Both words come from a Greek word meaning 'dwarf'.

nannicock [**nann**-ee-kock] an obsolete and rare word, so obsolete and rare the *OED* just notes its existence and does not give any meaning for it. The one citation is from 1600: "Hee that doth wonder at a Weathercocke . . . And is in loue with euery *Nannicocke*." Since there is no accepted meaning, please feel free to go forth and use it in any (mildly disparaging) sense you like.

naology [nay-**ah**-luh-djee] the study of churches, temples, and other sacred buildings. *Naometry* is the measurement of sacred buildings. From a Greek word meaning 'temple'.

naufragate [**naw**-fri-gate] an obsolete and rare verb meaning 'to wreck'. If something is *naufrageous*, it is in danger of shipwreck; if it is *naufragous*, it causes shipwreck. These all derive from a Latin word meaning 'to suffer shipwreck'.

nauscopy [**naw**-skuh-pee] the art of seeing the approach of ships or landfall from a considerable distance. The *OED* goes on to say "This pretended art was invented by a M. Bottineau . . . from the year 1782 to 1784." Bottineau claimed that he could see past the horizon by observing the effects that approaching ships had on the atmosphere. The governor of Mauritius requested that he keep a record of his predictions, and he successfully predicted the arrival of more than 550 ships, some as many as four days before they arrived. He turned down an offer of 3,000 francs for his secret and died in 1789.

nazar [**naz**-ahr] in India, a present made to a superior by an inferior, especially one made upon being introduced.

nidulation [nidj-oo-**lay**-shun] nesting or nest making. Also, *nidification*. A *nidifugous* bird is a bird that has young that are able to leave the nest immediately after birth. These words all come from a Latin word meaning 'nest'.

nittiness [**nit**-ee-nis] an obsolete word meaning 'the condition of being full of small air bubbles'. The one citation in the *OED* seems to be about wine.

NOBODADDY

Nobodaddy [**noh**-boh-dad-ee] a word used by William Blake as a disrespectful name for God. By extension, used for someone no longer admired. A blend of *nobody* and *daddy*.

nocency [**noh**-sun-see] an obsolete word meaning 'guilt'. This is the thing that *innocence* is the opposite of. Something that is *nocent* is harmful or criminal.

noceur [**naw**-sur] someone who stays up late at night. Also, 'a rake or libertine'. Rakes and libertines are hardly ever in their beds before ten. (Someone else's bed, sure, but not their own.) From a French word of the same meaning.

noctograph [**nock**-toh-graf] a tool for writing used by a blind person. The *noctograph* seems to have used an early form of carbon paper, with wires to guide the pen or stylus of the writer. The word also means 'a device or log to track the progress of night watchmen or guards on their rounds'. From Latin words meaning 'night' and 'writing'.

nod-crafty [**nahd**-kraf-tee] an adjective meaning 'able to nod with an air of great wisdom'. An essential characteristic of college professors and television talking heads and presenters.

notarikon [noh-**tarr**-i-kun] a word from kabbala, meaning 'the art of making a new word from the letters taken from the beginning (or middle, or end) of the words in a sentence'. A Greekification of a Latin word meaning 'shorthand writer'.

nudiustertian [n(y)oo-dee-uh-**stur**-shun] an obsolete and rare (yet incredibly useful) word meaning 'of the day before yesterday'. Used by extension also to mean 'the very newest'. From a Latin phrase meaning 'three days earlier'.

nullibicity [null-uh-**biss**-i-tee] a rare word meaning 'the condition of not existing anywhere'. The adjective is *nullibiquitous*. The *nullibicity* of certain information on the Internet continues to surprise and amaze many people, who assume that everything has been put up on the Web, somewhere. A *nullibist* is person who believes that a spirit or incorporeal being does not exist. From a Latin word meaning 'nowhere'.

obacerate [oh-**bass**-uh-rate] an obsolete and rare word meaning 'to contradict'. *Obaceration* is the action of shutting someone's mouth—whether metaphorically or physically is not clear.

obambulate [ob-**am**-byuh-late] a rare word meaning 'to walk about, wander'. *Obambulatory* is the adjective, meaning 'habitually walking around'. Most of the citations in the *OED* seem to refer to ghosts and spirits. From a Latin word meaning 'to walk'.

Ollendorffian [ah-lun-**dorf**-ee-un] an adjective meaning 'written in the artificial and overly formal style of foreign-language phrase books'. From the name of Heinrich Gottfried Ollendorff (1803–1865), a German grammarian and educator. Famous examples of such language include "Stop, the postilion has been struck by lightning!", "A man is drowning. Is there a life buoy, a rope, a grapnel at hand?", and "Unhand me Sir, for my husband, who is an Australian, awaits without." (Which last deserves several readings at different levels.) Perhaps the most absurd phrasebook is *English as She is Spoke: The new guide of the conversation in Portuguese and English in two parts*(1855), by Pedro Caroline and Jose da Fonseca, which includes this nearly incomprehensible sentence in its introduction: "We expect then, who the little book (for the care what we wrote him, and for her typographical correction) that may be worth the expectation of the studious persons, and especially of the Youth, at which we dedicate him particularly."

IMPLUVIOUS OMBRIFUGE

ombrifuge [**ahm**-bruh-fyoodj] a rare word meaning 'a rain shelter'. From a Greek word meaning 'a shower of rain'. A semantically related word is *paravent*, 'a wind shelter'.

omnifarious [ahm-ni-**fair**-ee-us] an adjective meaning 'dealing with all kinds of things' or 'of all kinds or forms'.

oneirocritical [oh-nye-roh-**krit**-i-cle] an adjective meaning 'expert in the interpretation of dreams'.

opsophagize [ahp-**sah**-fug-gize] to eat delicacies, especially fish. *Opsophagist* is the agent noun. From a Greek word of the same meaning.

oryctognosy [or-ick-**tog**-nuh-see] an obsolete word meaning 'knowledge of minerals'. From Greek words meaning 'dug up' and 'knowledge'.

oryzivorous [or-i-**ziv**-er-us] an adjective meaning 'rice eating'. As in "I used to be *oryzivorous,* but now I'm on that high-protein diet."

osphresiology [ahs-free-see-**ah**-luh-djee] the study of the sense of smell, or a scientific paper about smelling and scents. From a Greek word meaning 'smell'.

ostentiferous [ahs-tun-**tiff**-er-us] an obsolete and rare word meaning 'that which brings monsters or strange sights'. An *ostent* is a 'a sign or wonder, a portent'. From a Latin word meaning 'something shown'.

otenchyte [**oht**-n-kite] a tool or device for injecting liquid into the ears. Presumably for medicinal purposes, but it also sounds suitable as one of those "ways of making you talk." From Greek words meaning 'ear' and 'pour in'.

oultrepreu [oo-truh-**proo**] an obsolete and rare word meaning 'very brave'. From a French word meaning 'beyond brave'.

pactitious [pack-**tish**-us] an obsolete and rare adjective meaning 'characterized by being agreed upon or specified in a contract'.

paddereen [pad-er-**reen**] an Irish word meaning 'a bead of the rosary', and, figuratively, 'a bullet'. From a diminutive form of a word meaning 'the Lord's Prayer'.

paradiorthosis [parr-uh-dye-or-**thoh**-sis] an obsolete and rare word meaning 'a false correction'. Unfortunately, the practice of introducing errors into text that is already just fine is not as rare as this word.

parataxic [parr-uh-**tack**-sick] a term used by the psychologist H. S. Sullivan (1892–1949) to describe the condition in which subconscious attitudes or emotions affect relationships. A *parataxic distortion* is when you attribute traits of significant people in your past to people with whom you currently have a relationship. The opposite of *parataxis* is *syntaxis*, in which happy state objectivity and the use of 'consensually validated symbols' (in other words, things that both people agree upon the meaning of) are the basis for communication.

parorexia [parr-uh-**reck**-see-uh] an unnatural appetite, or an unnatural lack of appetite. A near synonym for *anorexia.*

pathognomy [path-**ahg**-nuh-mee] the study of the emotions, or the physical signs or expressions of them. A nice word that could possibly be extended to mean 'the study of tantrums'.

PECULIAR AND PREOCCUPYING PASTIMES

If you're bored with hide-and-seek, Go Fish, or *Doom*, you might want to try some of these entertaingly named games. Perhaps *able-whackets,* a card game where (according to the *OED*, quoting Smyth's *Sailor's Word-book*) the loser "is beaten over the palms of the hands with a handkerchief tightly twisted like a rope. Very popular with horny-fisted sailors." You could try *rythmomachy,* also called *the philosophers' game,* played with round, triangular, and square pieces, each marked with a number, on a board like two chessboards joined together. Robert Burton considered it a cure for melancholy.

If that sounds too much like work, there's always *cottabus,* an ancient Greek drinking game in which the goal was to throw wine from your cup into another container in a particular way (which seems the opposite of modern drinking games, in which the object is to get wine from your cup into you).

Many boy-and-girl games are defined in the *OED*, including *course-a-park,* a country game where a girl calls out a boy's name for him to chase her. (It's assumed that she doesn't try too hard not to be caught.) There's also *draw-glove,* where players race to take off their gloves (back when men and women wore gloves) at the mention of certain words. Winners tended to be awarded kisses. If, at a party, a double nut (called a *fillipeen*) was found by a lady, she gave one of the kernels to a gentleman to eat. Then, when they met again, each person tried to be the first to say "*Fillipeen!*" because the first one to say it was entitled to a present from the other.

Other games are more physical and less flirty. *Bumdockdousse* (also called *pimpompet*) is a game where you try to hit the other players on their rear ends with your feet. In *hinch-pinch,* one person hits another softly, the other player hits back with a little more force, and each subsequent blow in turn is harder, until it becomes a real fight. *Bumble-puppy* is essentially tetherball with a racket (but a *bumblepuppist* is someone who plays unscientific whist).

Kabaddi is a kind of pushing game popular in northern India and Pakistan, in which players have to hold their breath during their turns. (They prove this by saying "kabaddi"

> ***Bumble-puppy* is essentially tetherball with a racket (but a *bumblepuppist* is someone who plays unscientific whist).**

over and over again.) *Knappan* is an old Welsh game in which each side tries to drive a wooden ball as possible in one direction. One wonders if there was any practical limit on the distance, or if a very powerful team could find themselves miles from home at the end of the game!

Many games are underdefined or undefined, so that their object or goal is obscure. *Bubble-the-justice* is a 'game of nine holes'. *Warpling o' the green* is defined as 'a rustic game' (and sounds suspiciously like something out of *Cold Comfort Farm*). *Dingthrift, gresco, prelleds, penneech, rowland-hoe, sitisot,* and *whipperginnie* are all just defined with variants of "some game." It's a shame to have such good game-names go unused—feel free to make up your own rules and ludically reclaim them.

NIDIFUGOUS PEENGERS

peenge [peendj] to complain in a whining voice. One suspects that the qualification "in a whining voice" is unnecessary. Perhaps formed from *whinge*, and influenced by *peevish*.

pelotherapy [pee-loh-**therr**-uh-pee] medicinal mud baths or treatments. If these help you, you might be *pelophilous* ('mud loving'). From a Greek word meaning 'mud'.

peplos [**pep**-lahs] a shawl worn by women in ancient Greece, especially a ceremonial one woven yearly for the statue of Athena at Athens, which was embroidered with mythological subjects and carried in procession to her temple.

peramene [perr-uh-**meen**] an obsolete and rare adjective meaning 'very pleasant'.

percoarcted [per-koh-**ark**-tid] an obsolete and rare word meaning 'brought into a narrow room', useful for anyone who has ever had to move a large piece of furniture. *Coarct* is an obsolete verb meaning 'kept within narrow limits, restricted'.

percontation [per-kahn-**tay**-shun] a rare word meaning 'an inquiry'. The adjective is *percontatorial,* meaning 'inquisitive'. From a Latin word meaning 'to interrogate'.

percribrate [per-**krib**-rate] an obsolete and rare word meaning 'to sift'. From a Latin word meaning 'to sift thoroughly'. One of the citations in the *OED*, from 1668, is "Thy Brain thus blown up by the *percribrated* influence of thy moist Mistress, the Moon." Which, even sifted a few times, makes little sense out of context, and possibly not much more in context. This proves that even nonsense can be good enough to show the meaning of a word.

perculsion [per-**kull**-shun] a rare word meaning 'a severe shock, consternation'. From a Latin word meaning 'to upset'. Something that is *perculsive* gives you a shock.

percunctorily [per-**kungk**-ter-uh-lee] an obsolete word meaning 'lazily'. From a Latin word meaning 'to loiter', on the model of *perfunctorily*.

perhendinancer [per-**hen**-duh-nun-ser] a rare and obsolete word meaning 'a lodger, a traveler'. From a Latin word that literally means 'to defer until the day after tomorrow'.

pertainym [per-**tay**-nim] a name for an adjective that is usually defined with the phrase "of or pertaining to." *Abdominal, friarish,* and *heraldic* are all *pertainyms. Pertainyms* do not have antonyms. From *pertain* and the suffix *-nym,* meaning 'word'.

phenakism [**fen**-uh-kiz-um] a rare word meaning 'cheating, trickery'. From a Greek word meaning 'deception'.

philocomal [fi-**lah**-koh-mul] an adjective meaning 'characterized by love of or attention to the hair'.

phobanthropy [fah-**ban**-thruh-pee] the 'morbid dread of mankind'. From Greek words meaning 'fear' and 'man', influenced by *philanthropy.*

phoenicurous [fen-i-**kyoor**-us] an adjective that unfortunately does not mean 'taking care of phoenixes'. It means 'having a red tail'. From a Greek word meaning 'red tailed'.

phonascetics [foh-nuh-**set**-iks] a rare word for a kind of treatment for improving or strengthening the voice. From a Greek word meaning 'one who exercises the voice'.

phonendoscope [foh-**nen**-duh-scope] an instrument for amplifying small sounds of the human body, or within other solid bodies. Just in case you thought your stomach growling wasn't loud enough, you can use your handy *phonendoscope* and make sure the whole room hears. From Greek words meaning 'voice' and 'within'.

phonocamptics [foh-noh-**kamp**-ticks] the part of acoustics that deals with reflected sounds or echoes. From *phono-* plus a Greek word meaning 'to bend'.

pleonexia [plee-uh-**neck**-see-uh] greediness or avarice as a mental illness. From a Greek word meaning 'greed'. A similar adjective is *lucripetous*, 'eager for gain', which comes from a Latin word meaning 'to seek gain'.

plethysmograph [pli-**thiz**-muh-graff] an instrument that measures the changes in volume of a part of the body, especially changes in blood flow such as those caused by emotion. A citation from 1882 claims that "the *plethysmograph* . . . measures the amount of blood sent to the brain in any particular process of thought, and records the exact time for each process." It seems as if in the early days this was very uncomfortable, as the *plethysmograph* was described as "a rigid airtight container enclosing the subject entirely except for [the] head and neck."

plevisable [**plev**-iss-uh-bul] an obsolete law term meaning 'able to be bailed out'. From a French word meaning 'to warrant'.

ploddeill [plah-**deal**] an obsolete and rare word meaning 'a band of cudgelers'. (The *OED* marks this word as 'contemptuous', although I don't know how contemptuous the average dictionary editor would be if faced with a band of men carrying cudgels.)

plongeur [plahn-**zhoor**] a superior word for a dishwasher in a hotel or restaurant. The *OED* has this citation from the *Daily Telegraph*, from 1977: "Titles are nice but surely the Dorchester is going a little too far advertising for a 'Supervisor Plongeur' to head the washing up department."

pneobiognosis [puh-nee-oh-bye-og-**noh**-siss] a rare medico-legal word for a test used to prove whether a child was born alive or dead, based on the presence or absence of air in the lungs. From Greek words meaning 'life' and 'knowledge'.

pococurantish [poh-koh-koo-**rahn**-tish] an adjective meaning care-less or indifferent. From Latin words meaning 'little' and 'care'.

polydipsia [pah-lee-**dip**-see-uh] abnormally great thirst. Also used figuratively, as in "a *polydipsia* for fame." From a Greek word meaning 'very thirsty'.

PSYCHOPOMP

psychopomp [**sye**-koh-pomp] someone or something that leads souls to the place of the dead. Also, a spiritual guide for a (living) person's soul; a person who acts as a guide of a soul. From Greek words meaning 'soul' and 'guide'. The adjective is *psychopompous*, but somehow that seems to demand a different definition.

pug-nozzle [**pug**-nozz-zle] to move the nostrils and upper lip in the manner of a pug dog.

quader [**kway**-der] an obsolete and rare word meaning 'to square a number'.

quadragenarian [kwah-druh-djuh-**nair**-ee-un] someone who is forty years old. One such person is described as "a stalwart well-oiled *quadragenarian*" in an *OED* citation from 1892. The adjective is *quadragenarious*, which is used in the 1895 citation "One of these plumply mellow *quadrigenarious* bodies."

quadragesimarian [kwah-druh-djess-uh-**mair**-ee-un] an obsolete and rare word meaning 'someone who observes Lent'. This certainly applies to those people who observe Lent only as an opportunity for Friday fish fries as well as to those who take the more traditional and spiritual ascetic approach. The adjective *quaresimal* means 'having the qualities of Lenten fare; meager, austere'.

quadrumanous [kwah-**drum**-uh-nus] an adjective meaning 'apelike in destructiveness'. From a Latin word meaning 'four-handed (like an ape)'.

quaestuary [**kwess**-choo-err-ee] an adjective meaning 'money making'. Look for this word to show up in spam E-mail any minute now.

quagswag [**kwag**-swag] an obsolete and rare word meaning 'to shake back and forth'.

QUAGSWAGGING A NACKET

quar [kwor] an obsolete word meaning 'to choke or fill up (a channel or passage)'. Anyone who has a narrow hallway that seems to collect every random bicycle, awkward pair of shoes, and child's toy possible has a use for this word.

quatervois [kwah-ter-**vwah**] an obsolete and rare word meaning 'a crossroads, a place where four ways meet'. Influenced by French words meaning 'four' and 'way'.

raccolta [ruh-**kohl**-tuh] an obsolete word meaning 'a collection, a crop or harvest'. From an Italian word meaning 'to collect'.

rachisagra [rack-uh-**sag**-ruh] pain in the spine. From a Greek word meaning 'spine'.

rackensak [**rack**-in-sack] a possibly obsolete word meaning 'a native of Arkansas'.

rataplan [rat-uh-**plan**] a drumming noise. A verb, it means 'to beat a drum'. From an onomatopoeic French word of the same meaning.

ratomorphic [rat-oh-**mor**-fick] a rare word meaning 'someone who refuses to believe that people have any mental processes that can't be shown to exist in lower animals'. From *rat*, on the model of *anthropomorphic*.

ravigote [rah-vee-**gawt**] the herbs tarragon, chervil, chives, and burnet, which, when used together, were supposed to have the power of resuscitation. From a French word meaning 'to invigorate'.

relexification [ree-leck-si-fi-**kay**-shun] a term from linguistics that means 'the process of replacing a word or phrase in one language with the corresponding word or phrase from another language, without changing the grammar of the items introduced'. "I am *très* impressed" is an example of *relexification* of the French word *très* into English.

REMEMBLE

rememble [ri-**mem**-ble] a false memory, especially of some place, object, or event of one's childhood. Also used as a verb: "I *remembled* the house as being bigger, and not so yellow." Possibly a blend of 'fumble' and 'remember'. This word was coined by Elan Cole, who suggested it on the radio show *The Next Big Thing*.

rhineurynter [**rine**-yoo-rin-ter] an inflatable bag used to plug the nose. This seems to have some medical application, and is not, as one might think, a murder weapon or an instrument of torture. It comes from Greek words meaning 'nose' and 'to broaden'.

rhyparographer [rip-uh-**rah**-gruh-fer] a painter of unpleasant or sordid subjects. From Greek words meaning 'filthy' and 'writer'.

RHYPAROGRAPHER

I call it "Mom"

rhytidectomy [rye-ti-**deck**-tuh-mee] the surgical removal of wrinkles, especially from the face. Used also as a technical term for 'face-lift'. From Greek words meaning 'wrinkle' and 'cutting'.

ribaldail [**rib**-ul-dale] an obsolete word meaning 'common fellows, low company'. From the same (obscure) root as *ribald*. In the royal household of France there used to be an officer called the *king of the ribalds,* who had jurisdiction over all the brothels and gaming houses around the court.

ribazuba [ree-buh-**zoo**-buh] an obsolete word for walrus ivory. From Russian words meaning 'fish' and 'tooth'.

rimbombo [rim-**bahm**-boh] a rare word meaning 'a booming roar'. To *rimbomb* is 'to echo or resound'.

rixation [rick-**say**-shun] an obsolete word meaning 'scolding, fighting'. From a Latin word meaning 'to quarrel'.

rockoon [rah-**koon**] a rocket fired from a balloon, or a balloon carrying a rocket. A blend of *rocket* and *balloon.*

roinish [**roy**-nish] an obsolete word meaning 'scabby, coarse, despicable'. *Roin* is an obsolete word meaning 'scab'.

rosicler [**rose**-ik-clear] the rosy light of dawn.

roucoulement [roo-cool-**mahn**] a rare word meaning 'the gentle cooing of doves', of course also extended to mean the soft voices of women. From a French word of the same meaning.

S

Sabaism [**say**-bay-iz-um] the worship and adoration of the stars. From a Hebrew word meaning 'host'.

salebrosity [sal-uh-**brah**-si-tee] 'unevenness, roughness'. From a Latin word of the same meaning.

samentale [**sah**-mun-tale] a obsolete word meaning 'agreement'. It seems to come from the phrase 'of the same tale'.

sandapile [san-**dah**-puh-lee] an obsolete word meaning 'a coffin'.

sanguinolency [sang-**gwin**-uh-lun-see] an obsolete word meaning 'addiction to bloodshed'. Thankfully, most of the *sanguinolent* these days can satisfy their jones for gore with video games and movies. From a Latin word meaning 'blood'.

sarcinarious [sahr-si-**nair**-ee-us] an obsolete word meaning 'able to carry burdens or loads'. From a Latin word meaning 'bundle'.

Sardanapalian [sahrd-nuh-**pay**-lee-un] an adjective meaning 'luxuriously effeminate'. From the name of Sardanapalus, the last king of Nineveh, who was supposed to have lived in outrageous luxury. Beseiged by the Medes for two years, his favorite concubine induced him to put himself on a funeral pyre. She set fire to it herself and it consumed the palace and his entire court. The legend of Sardanapalus cannot be connected with any Assyrian king known through archaeology.

Sardoodledom [sahr-**doo**-dle-dum] a word used to describe well-written and clever, but trivial or immoral, plays, or the milieu in which such work is praised. From the name of French playwright Victorien Sardou (1831–1908). His best-known farce is *Divorçons (Let's Get a Divorce)* (1880), in which a married woman, hearing about a new divorce law about to be passed, starts a flirtation with her husband's cousin. The cousin deceives her with a telegram, implying that the law has been passed. The woman then suggests a friendly divorce to her husband, who agrees and resumes his bachelor life, which makes the woman jealous. The woman and her husband dine in private together and reconcile, leaving the cousin alone and discomfited.

sarvodaya [sahr-**voh**-dah-yah] a word meaning 'the well-being of all'. Used by Gandhi (1869–1948) to mean a new social order without caste, based on nonviolence and service. From a Sanskrit word meaning 'prosperity'.

Satanophany [say-tuh-**nah**-fuh-nee] a visible manifestation of Satan. From *Satan*, obviously, and the same *-phany* as in *epiphany*, from a Greek word meaning 'manifestation'.

satisdiction [sat-is-**dick**-shun] a word meaning 'saying enough'. If only we knew to shut up after achieving *satisdiction*. From Latin words meaning 'enough' and 'saying', on the model of *satisfaction*. Another 'enough' word is *satispassion*, which means 'atonement by adequate suffering', which leads to the burning question: "How much suffering is enough?" Especially the suffering caused by someone who never seems to reach *satisdiction*.

scabilonian [skab-uh-**loh**-nee-un] the *OED* glosses this word as 'a contemptuous term for some kind of garment'.

scacchic [**skack**-kick] a rare adjective meaning 'of or pertaining to chess'. From an Italian word meaning 'chess'.

scelestious [si-**less**-chus] a rare adjective meaning 'wicked'. Another form is *scelestic*. They both come from a Latin word with the same meaning.

schismogenesis [sizz-moh-**jen**-uh-sis] the differentiation between people, social groups, or cultures caused by reciprocal exaggerated responses to each other's behavior. Everyone is familiar with the classic relationship example: one person has a fear of abandonment, the other a fear of commitment, and every advance in intimacy is met by a pulling back, leading to more pursuit and many, many bad romantic comedies. Falling in love can be considered a kind of inverted *schismogenesis;* instead of differentiation, assimilation. From a Greek word meaning 'rift, cleft' and -*genesis*.

Schrecklichkeit [**shreck**-likh-ite] a deliberate policy of terrorizing non-combatants. Sometimes used figuratively, as in this citation from 1977: "The Schrecklichkeit in which the relations between parents and children are so often conducted in Britain."

scevity [**see**-vuh-tee] an obsolete word meaning 'unluckiness'. It comes (like so many "unlucky" words do) from a Latin word with a 'left' meaning—in this case 'left-sided, awkward'.

sciapodous [sye-**app**-uh-dus] having feet large enough to shelter the whole body when used as an umbrella. From a Greek word meaning 'shadow foot'. The *Sciapodes* who had these feet were supposed to live in Libya.

scolecophagous [skah-li-**koff**-uh-gus] worm eating. Used mostly about birds (especially early ones) but ripe for extended, metaphorical, or figurative use.

scollardicall [skuh-**lahr**-di-kle] an adjective supposed to be an illiterate epithet for a learned person.

scopperloit [**skah**-per-loit] a time for play, or rude or rough-housing play. Of obscure origin.

scoteography [skoh-tee-**ogg**-ruh-fee] the art of writing in the dark. From Greek words meaning 'darkness' and 'writing'.

scriniary [**skrye**-nee-err-ee] a keeper of the archives, an archivist. From a Latin word meaning 'a box for books and papers; a writing desk'.

scriptitation [skrip-ti-**tay**-shun] an obsolete and rare word meaning 'continuous writing'. From a Latin word meaning 'to write'. *Scriptitation* is what you wish your favorite authors would do.

semihiant [sem-ee-**hye**-unt] an adjective meaning '(of lips) half-open'. Much, much nicer than *agape* or *slack-jawed*. The one citation for this word in the *OED* shows that it's very nice: "He stooped and kissed the *semihiant* lips."

sengilbond [**seng**-gul-bond] an obsolete and rare word meaning 'an encircling band'. Someone should snap this up as a trade name for those plastic straps that hold shipping cartons shut—the ones that are nearly impossible to remove unless you attempt to use them as carrying handles, in which case they disobligingly snap open immediately.

SINGERIE

singerie [san-zhuh-**ree**] a decorative style using pictures of monkeys, often wearing clothes or indulging in other anthropomorphic behavior. From a French word meaning 'monkey business; a collection of monkeys'.

STRANGE AND SENSATIONAL SERVANTS

If words are the servants of thoughts, words for servants should serve some weird and wonderful thinking, if only of the "why?", "how?", and "huh?" variety.

Harlots are attended by their *apple-squires,* and greyhounds by their *fewterers;* ship's surgeons have their *loblolly boys,* and Roman magistrates their *apparitors.* Indian landowners have a *chuprassy* or two hanging around, wearing their official badges in splendor, and every bluestocking employs a *lectrice* to read aloud. Scholars and magicians have at least one *famulus,* to keep the place suitably untidy and obtain impossible things at short notice. A bullfighter has a *mozo,* and a priest has a *crucifer* to do the heavy lifting of carrying a cross in procession.

Someone who attends a bedchamber is a *cubicular;* someone who attends a bath is a *topass.* Someone who cuts your bread at the table is a *trenchpaine.* The *scrape-trencher* did just that. In India, the head of your pantry and kitchen is a *khansamah,* and a general table servant is a *khidmutgar.* The *squiller* is in charge of the scullery. A *mediastine* is a kitchen drudge. The *manciple* purchases provisions for a college or a monastery.

Military attendants, or those dressed in military or huntsman style, like *chasseurs* and *jaegers,* are always popular. *Escuderos* bear shields, or are ladies' pages; a *coistrel* is in charge of the horses of a knight (and is also a 'low varlet'). If you want your servant to run secret errands, wearing gray instead of your normal livery, you have a *grison* in your employ. An armed courier (especially in Turkey) is a *kavass*. A *pandour* is much the same, only in Croatia and Hungary. A *wanlasour* drives the game back toward you for ease of shooting. A *ferash* will spread your carpet and pitch your tent, among other things. A *piqueur* will run before your carriage to clear the road. A *syce* will tend to your horses and follow your carriage on foot. A *mussalchee* will carry a torch for you (but only in the literal sense).

If you just need a general servant, you can hire an *attendress*, an *underlout*, a *backman* or *jackman*, a *knape*, a *tindal*, a *pedissequent*, a *valect*, or (if you want one for unscrupulous duties only) a *myrmidon*. Where do you find your servants, especially your *schelchenes*, or

> **Scholars and magicians have at least one *famulus*, to keep the place suitably untidy and obtain impossible things at short notice.**

servant girls? Well, you can try your local *giglet-fair*. Don't forget to pay them their *arles*, or hiring bonus, to confirm their engagement. They will expect to have their *kist*, or trunk, sent for as well.

slangrel [**slang**-grul] an obsolete and rare word meaning 'a lean or long person or thing'.

solfeggist [sol-**fedj**-ist] someone who sings notes using do (or ut), re, mi, fa, sol, la, and si (or ti). From the names of the notes *sol* and *fa*.

spanghew [**spang**-hyoo] to cause a frog or toad to fly into the air. (Usually violently, from the end of a stick, although it seems as though it wouldn't ever feel gentle to the poor toad or frog!) Of obscure origin.

spartle [**spahr**-tul] a Scottish word meaning 'to move the body in a sprawling or struggling way, to thrash around'.

sparto-statics [**spahr**-toh-stat-icks] the study of the strength of ropes. Since there is only one citation in the *OED* for this word, it's amusing to imagine the melodramatic death of the would-be sparto-statician, who, having misjudged a particular rope's strength, goes plummeting over the cliff.

spawling [**spawl**-ing] an archaic word for the act of spitting, or the results of spitting. The word *spawl* means 'to spit copiously'.

stafador [**staff**-uh-dore] a obsolete and rare word meaning 'an impostor'. From a Spanish word meaning 'to swindle'.

stenotopic [sten-uh-**top**-ik] an adjective meaning 'able to tolerate only a restricted range of ecological conditions or habitats'. So your relative who must have the window open exactly five inches and who cannot eat anything but plain chicken breast and steamed broccoli? *Stenotopic.*

storiation [stor-ee-**ay**-shun] decoration of something with designs that represent historical, legendary, or symbolic subjects. Practically every public mural has some kind of *storiation*.

subumber [sub-**um**-ber] an obsolete and rare word meaning 'to shelter'. However, the word *subumbrage* means 'to overshadow'. Both words are related to *umbrella*, and come from a Latin word meaning 'shade'.

sudorific [soo-duh-**riff**-ik] an adjective meaning 'causing perspiration', either through effort or in a medical way. Also, thankfully more rarely, 'consisting of sweat'.

surbater [sur-**bay**-ter] an obsolete and rare word for 'someone who tires another person with walking'. According to most young children, all parents are *surbaters*.

surfle [**sur**-fle] a face wash or cosmetic. Obviously predating the development of product naming or brand awareness. *Surfle* can also mean 'to embroider', and comes from a Latin word that means 'thread on top'.

sursaut [sur-**sawt**] in the phrase *a sursaut* this means 'all of a sudden'. Also, as a verb, 'to attack suddenly'. From a Latin word meaning 'leap'.

swabble [**swah**-ble] to make a noise like water being sloshed around.

swanimote [**swah**-nuh-mote] a special court, formerly held fifteen days before Michaelmas. It was originally one where forest officers superintended the departure of pigs and cattle and sheep from the king's woods so that they didn't interfere with the hunting. From a Latin word meaning 'a meeting of swineherds'.

swan-upping [**swahn**-up-ing] the task of marking swans by nicking their beaks, to brand them as being owned by the crown or a company.

swartrutter [**swort**-rut-er] a mercenary soldier who wore black clothes and armor and blackened his face. The *OED* notes that they "infested the Netherlands in the 16th and 17th centuries." Literally, 'black trooper'.

swasivious [sway-**siv**-ee-us] an obsolete or rare word meaning 'agreeably persuasive'. Much better than being disagreeably persuasive, in the action-movie, gun-to-the-head way.

swayamvara [sway-ahm-**vah**-ruh] a Hindu ceremony in which a woman chooses her husband from several candidates, or a symbolic version of this before an arranged marriage. The girl signals her choice by giving him a garland of flowers. From Sanskrit words meaning 'self choice'.

swazzle [**swah**-zle] a mouthpiece used by a puppeteer to make the squeaking voice of Mr. Punch.

sweeny [**swee**-nee] a word meaning 'atrophy of the shoulder (in a horse)' but used figuratively to mean 'stiff with pride or self-importance'. From a German word meaning 'atrophy'.

T

testudineous [tes-t(y)oo-**din**-ee-us] an adjective meaning 'as slow as a tortoise'. From a Latin word meaning 'tortoise'.

theoplasm [**thee**-oh-plaz-um] a rare word meaning 'the stuff of which gods are made'.

tranlace [tran-**lace**] to repeat a word in the shape of its cognates or derivatives, especially as wordplay or as a rhetorical device: "My message, my premise, my commission are all the same, and I submit them to you, with my promise, as a missionary, to omit nothing."

transume [tran-**soom**] to make an official copy of a document, usually a legal document.

trichechine [**trick**-i-kine] an adjective meaning 'like a walrus (or manatee)'. It comes from the modern Latin name of a genus (no longer used) including the manatee and walrus, from Greek roots meaning 'having hair'. A good adjective for a particular kind of unfortunate moustache.

truandal [true-un-**dall**] a plural noun meaning 'beggars or camp-followers'. From an Old French word meaning 'an assemblage of beggars'.

Turlupin [ter-**loo**-pin] the name for a group of fourteenth-century heretics who believed that one shouldn't be ashamed of anything that is natural. A good word for those who seek to excuse their bad manners or bad behavior with the excuse "everybody does it!"

tutoyant [too-twah-**yah**] an adjective meaning 'intimate, affectionate'. *Tutoyer* means 'to use the familiar pronoun *tu* or *thou*', or 'to *tu* or *thou* someone'.

tyrotoxism [tye-roh-**tock**-siz-um] cheese-poisoning. This particular ptomaine (diazobenzene hyrdroxide) can also be found in bad milk. From Greek words meaning 'cheese' and 'poison'.

ubiquarian [yoo-bi-**kwair**-ee-un] a rare word meaning 'a person who goes everywhere'.

uliginous [yoo-**lidj**-uh-nus] an adjective meaning 'swampy, slimy, oozy'. From a Latin word meaning 'full of moisture'.

umberment [**um**-ber-mint] an obsolete word meaning 'a number, a multitude'.

umbratile [**um**-bruh-tile] an adjective meaning 'spent inside or indoors; private, not public'. From a Latin word meaning 'keeping in the shade'. The noun *umbratile* means 'a person who spends his time in the shade' with the connotation 'lazy'.

umtagati [oom-tah-**gah**-tee] a South African word (from Nguni) meaning 'a wizard or witch; a worker of evil magic'.

unwelewable [un-**well**-yoo-uh-ble] an obsolete and rare adjective that means 'unfadable'. This word is related to an obsolete *wallow*, meaning 'to fade away, to waste'.

upbigged [up-**bigd**] a Scots word meaning 'built up'. A more suitable word for strip-mall sprawl could not be found.

UBIQUARIAN

uranography [yoo-ruh-**nah**-gruh-fee] a rare and obsolete word meaning 'a description of heaven'. From Greek roots meaning 'heaven' and 'writing'.

verticordious [ver-ti-**kor**-dee-us] an obsolete and rare word that means 'turning the heart from evil'. From a Latin word meaning 'turner of hearts', used as an epithet for Venus.

viron [**vye**-run] an obsolete word meaning 'to go around, to make the circuit'. Useful as another word to mean 'going in circles'. From an Old French word meaning 'to turn'.

visagiste [vee-zuh-**zheest**] a makeup artist. From a French word with the same meaning.

visceration [vis-uh-**ray**-shun] a rare word meaning 'a portion of raw flesh, especially one distributed at the death of a rich man'. It's assumed that the flesh is that of an animal, and not that of the rich man. Related to the word *viscera*.

viscerotonic [vis-uh-roh-**tah**-nick] having a sociable, easy-going, comfort-seeking personality, usually associated with an endomorphic body type.

voculation [vock-yuh-**lay**-shun] a rare word meaning 'correct pronunciation and enunciation, giving every word its correct accent, moderation, and measure'. From a Latin word meaning 'little voice'. Also from this Latin word is *vocule*, the faint final sound heard when pronouncing certain consonants.

VISAGISTE of the BLOTTESQUE

volacious [voh-**lay**-shus] suitable for flying. Something that has the power of flight is *volitorial*. From a Latin word meaning 'to fly'. With the heightened awareness of security in airports lately, this word might come in handy.

volpone [vahl-**poh**-nee] a cunning schemer, a miser. From the name of the main character in Ben Jonson's (1572–1637) play *Volpone, or the Fox* (1606), in which Volpone himself says "What a rare punishment / Is avarice to itself." *Volpone* is an Italian word for 'fox'.

vomer [**voh**-mer] a small bone that is part of the partition between the nostrils in humans and most vertebrates. From a Latin word meaning 'plowshare'.

BOGGLISH WAVENGER

wahala [wuh-**hah**-luh] (in Nigeria) inconvenience, trouble, fuss, calamity. From Hausa.

wavenger [**way**-vin-djer] an obsolete word meaning 'a stray animal'. Possibly from *waif*, with the ending modeled after the *-enger* of *passenger*, *scavenger*, etc.

whelve [whelv] an obsolete word meaning 'to turn something over and hide something beneath it' or 'to bury something'. To *whelve over* is to overwhelm.

whistness [**whist**-nis] an obsolete word meaning 'silence'. Of onomatopoeic origin, related to *hush!* and *hist!*

widdiful [**wid**-i-full] someone who deserves hanging. Another word with this meaning is *waghalter*. From *widdy*, 'a rope for hanging'.

windlestraw [**win**-dle-straw] a tall, thin, unhealthy-looking person.

winx [wingks] an obsolete word meaning 'to bray like an ass'. If you'd rather sound like the other laughing animal, the hyena, the word for making that sound is *hau-hau*.

XYZ

xenelasy [zen-**nee**-luh-see] a law in ancient Sparta by which foreigners could be expelled at any time. The classical city-state equivalent of "the management reserves the right to refuse service to anyone." From Greek words meaning 'foreigner' and 'drive away'.

xenomenia [zen-oh-**mee**-nee-uh] a medical condition in which blood flows from some part of a woman's body at a different place than (but at the same time as, and replacing) her regular menses. Also called 'vicarious menstruation'. From Greek words meaning 'strange' and 'menses'.

xylopyrography [zye-loh-pye-**rah**-gruh-fee] the art of creating designs on wood with a hot poker or wire. (The word "art" here should probably be in quotation marks, or at least read with air quotes.) A marvelous way of intentionally ruining perfectly good furniture.

yaply [**yap**-lee] an adverb meaning 'eagerly, hungrily'. *Yapness* is a noun meaning 'hunger', and *yap*, obviously, means 'hungry'.

yemeles [**yeem**-lis] an obsolete word meaning 'careless, negligent'. To *take yeme* is to observe or be careful.

yerd-hunger [**yurd**-hung-ger] an overwhelming desire for food, sometimes found in people near death.

yesterfang [**yes**-ter-fang] something that was caught or taken yesterday.

yisel [**yiss**-ul] an obsolete word meaning 'a hostage'.

youf [yowf] to bark in a muffled way.

zabernism [**zab**-er-niz-um] an obsolete word meaning 'the abuse of military power or authority; unjustified aggression'. From the name *Zabern*, the German name for Saverne in Alsace, where in 1912 an overeager German subaltern killed a cobbler who smiled at him.

zeitgeber [**tsite**-gebb-er] a cyclical event in the environment, especially one that acts as a cue for biological rhythms in an organism. From German words meaning 'time' and 'giver'.

zendik [**zen**-dick] a person "in the East" who not only doesn't believe in the accepted religion, but who has also been accused of "magical heresy".

zenocratically [zee-nuh-**krat**-ik-lee] with the authority of Zeus or Jove.

zizany [**ziz**-uh-nee] an obsolete word meaning 'a harmful weed', also used figuratively in the sense 'a bad apple (that spoils the barrel)'.

zoilist [**zoy**-list] a critic, especially one who is unduly severe or who takes joy in faultfinding. From the name of Zoilus (*c*.400–*c*.320BC), an ancient Greek who managed to criticize both Homer and Plato.

zoonosis [zoh-uh-**noh**-sis] a disease transmitted to people by animals, like rabies. From Greek words meaning 'animal' and 'disease'.

FINDING NEW WEIRD AND WONDERFUL WORDS

You're reading your favorite magazine, a new novel, or your local paper, and you come across this sentence: "It was an eerie, crebadative feeling, as if she were being watched." *Crebadative?* you wonder. You check a dictionary (or two, or three) and you don't find it. What you have found is a new word. A classic new word, one that has a completely different arrangement of letters from any other existing word. You understand roughly what it means, from context, but you're not sure, and you file it away in your head as new and unusual. You probably won't write it or speak it yourself, unless you're very playful or adventurous—you don't have firm grasp on it, and there are plenty of other words in your storehouse that you feel more comfortable with. A little later, perhaps, you read this sentence: "Scientists in Melbourne have discovered a new enzyme responsible for fat digestion, lipafazil." *Lipafazil?* You probably don't check that one at all, slotting it instead into a neat compartment in your brain labeled "science stuff." And you don't use it (unless you yourself are an enzyme-research scientist) because you simply have no need for it.

This kind of new-word-finding experience is what most people think of when they (or if they) think about new words: the unique word appearing out of the blue, especially the unique science or technology word. This kind of new word is often called "coined," and in some cases a particular person can be credited with the invention of the word (as with the word *cyberspace*, which was coined by William Gibson in 1982). Even coined words, though, aren't usually completely original combinations of letters; a combination like *phygrttle* is certainly original, but it looks hard to pronounce and doesn't give readers any clue as to what it means, unlike the word *infomercial,* which is a readily recognizable "blend" of *information* and *commercial.* Many coined words are blended from two already accepted words. One completely original coined word is *googol* ('ten raised to the hundredth power [10^{100}]'), which was invented by the nine-year-old nephew of a mathematician.

However, from the lexicographer's point of view, most new words aren't the careful coinage of a single person, or even the simultaneous independent coinages of several people (which happens more often than you might think, to the frustration of all involved). Many new words are stolen by English from other languages; words like *keiretsu,* from Japanese, or *chicano,* from Mexican Spanish. English is very likely to swipe words for food: *chianti, sauerkraut, tandoori.* Sometimes English, instead of taking the word, just transmutes the foreign word into English. German *Übermensch,* for example, became English *superman.* This is called a *calque* (from the French for 'copy') or a *loan translation.* Occasionally, people will hear foreign or unfamiliar words and reanalyze them to fit them into a more familiar form, making new words. This process is called *folk etymology,* and made words like *cockroach,* from Spanish *cucaracha,* and *woodchuck,* from an Algonquian word often spelled *otchek.* Occasionally this process is more involved, as with *alligator pear,* 'avocado'—given this name because they were supposed to grow where alligators were common.

New acronyms are very common, and occasionally become words whose acronymic origins are all but forgotten by users (words like *scuba,* 'self-contained underwater breathing apparatus', and *snafu,* 'situation normal, all (fouled) up', rarely come across as acronyms today, and the origin of a word like *gigaflops*, where the *-flops* is from 'floating-point operations per second' is not blatantly acronymic). There is even a recent trend toward making *bacronyms*, words that are made acronymically but for which the most important consideration is that the acronym make an appropriate (usually already existing) word or phrase, such as MADD, 'Mothers Against Drunk Driving', or the recent USA-PATRIOT Act, in which USA-PATRIOT stands for 'Uniting and Strengthening America by Providing Appropriate Tools Required to Intercept and Obstruct Terrorism'.

Although entirely new words are exciting to the lexicographer and the layperson alike, changes to existing words can thrill as well. The meanings of words are no more fixed than any other aspect of human culture, and despite well-meaning efforts by many to make them stand still, they continue to change. Spotting these new meanings takes a more sophisticated approach to language, and one that is more sensitized to shades of definition instead of just knee-jerkishly categorizing a new meaning as "wrong."

A favorite kind of lexical change is metaphorical extension: the computer meanings of *mouse* and *virus* are good examples of this, as is the basketball meaning of *dunk*. An unfavorite, though frequent, kind of lexical change is change in grammatical function, for example the verbing of nouns. Why one kind of change is welcomed and thought clever by logophiles while the other kind is deplored and thought degrading is unclear, but *impact, contact, script, conference,* and other verbs-from-nouns are in very frequent use.

Words' meanings can get worse, a process called *pejoration;* this has happened in a big way to words like *barefaced,* which originally meant just 'open, unconcealed', and then became 'shameless', and in a small way to words like *poetess* and *actress*, which now seem like lightweights compared to *poet* and *actor*. Words can also improve their meanings, or *ameliorate*. The word *luxury* originally meant 'lust', but gradually changed to mean 'something desirable but not indispensable'.

Besides getting better or worse, meanings can become more or less inclusive. Becoming less inclusive is called *specialization,* as when *amputate* went from meaning 'to cut off' to meaning 'to cut off a limb or other part of the body'. Becoming more inclusive is called *generalization,* as when the word *pants* went from meaning specifically 'pantaloons' to meaning (in the U. S. at least) almost any kind of lower-body covering.

Some new words are just shorter versions of old words. These are made either through *clipping* (*fax* from *facsimile, exam* from *examination* are standard examples) or from *back formation* (*burgle* from *burglar, bus* from *busboy, edit* from *editor*). This is so common that most people don't register these words as "new" or are astonished to learn that the longer word is older. This is probably because many other new words are formed by *derivation,* that is, by adding affixes to existing words, lengthening them. (*Affixes* are prefixes and suffixes, and, in facetious use only, infixes, which are parts inserted in the middle of words. Infixes are usually only used with obscenities: *abso-frickin'-lutely.*) Words like *ascertainable* and *finalization* are derivatives. Many of the new words added to dictionaries are derivatives, added to the end of existing entries.

Words made from proper names are called *eponyms: sequoia* and *silhouette* are two well-known examples. Using a proper name to stand for something having an attribute associated with that name is called *antonomasia,* and calling someone especially perspicacious a *Sherlock* is one example. When proper names are treated in this way they are very often added to dictionaries and thus count, for lexicographical purposes, as new words. The genericization of trademarks (like *thermos* and *aspirin*) also falls under antonomasia.

One last method of forming new words is *echoing,* or *onomatopoeia,* in which new words are made to resemble real-world sounds, like *bleep, bloop,* and *boing!* This might be the most fun way to make new words, but it is also less likely to create words that give off that "new" feel, especially if the sound is familiar.

With this field guide to word formation processes you should now be able to find new words everywhere you look—and possibly create a few yourself.

A WEBLIOGRAPHY OF WEIRD AND WONDERFUL WORD SITES

The World Wide Web is well served by sites that feature the English language, especially its history and its peculiarities of vocabulary. Some of the better known and more popular ones are listed here. None concentrate exclusively on weird words, though they often form part of the mix.

MAILING LISTS

A Word A Day   <http://www.wordsmith.org/awad/subscribe.html>
Anu Garg's list is the granddaddy of online words' mailing lists, now with more than half a million subscribers. A new word is sent out every weekday.

Merriam-Webster's Word of the Day
                          <http://www.m-w.com/service/subinst.htm>
A free seven-day-a-week service featuring a word, with a commentary, taken from the publisher's Unabridged Dictionary.

Garner's Usage Tip of the Day
                  <http://www.oup-usa.org/mailman/listinfo/us-usage-l>
A free five-day-a-week service featuring a usage tip from Bryan Garner, author of *Modern American Usage*.

Vocabulary Mail   <http://www.vocabularymail.com>
A daily mailing, featuring between one and three words. The emphasis is on building one's vocabulary.

Word of the Day   <http://www.dictionary.com/wordoftheday/list/>
Another seven-day-a-week service which is strongly biased towards vocabulary building, so usually features workaday words rather than weird ones.

Word Spy   <www.logophilia.com/WordSpy/subscribe.html>
Each weekday, Paul McFedries chooses a term culled from newspapers and magazines. The emphasis is on neologisms, so many of the choices reflect journalists' inventive wordsmithery.

World Wide Words   <http://www.worldwidewords.org/>
Michael Quinion writes on words from a British standpoint; his weekly e-mail newsletter is linked to a Web site, one of whose sections is actually called Weird Words.

Other regular dictionary definitions are featured on the *Oxford English Dictionary* and *AskOxford* sites—see below.

REGULAR WEB COLUMNS

OED Word of the Day   <http://www.oed.com/cgi/display/wotd>
Each daily word page consists of its full *Oxford English Dictionary* definition, with all its sub-senses and examples.

Take Our Word For It   <http://www.takeourword.com/>
Melanie & Mike discuss word etymologies, often of unusual, outmoded, or weird words. The site is updated weekly and you can get additional material and news of changes by joining a mailing list.

Word Detective   <http://www.word-detective.com/>
This is the Web archive of pieces on word history by Evan Morris which appear in his syndicated newspaper columns. Updated every month.

WRITINGS ON WORDS

Ask Oxford   <http://www.askoxford.com/>
A British-based compendium of information about words, including Word of the Day, Quote of the Week, Ask the Experts, and word games.

Martha Barnette's Fun Words   <http://www.funwords.com/>
An entertaining compendium of quirky words.

Mavens' Word of the Day   <http://www.randomhouse.com/wotd/>
From the Word Mavens of Random House. This has now closed, but an archive of past pieces gives answers to queries about the meanings of words and expressions, many of them acceptably weird.

Urban Legends Archive
              <http://www.urbanlegends.com/language/etymology/>
This discusses, and debunks, some of the stranger stories about the origins of words that circulate online and off.

Verbatim   <http://www.verbatimmag.com/>
The online archive for the quarterly magazine which investigates the (often odd) byways of language.

Vocabula Review   <http://www.vocabula.com/>
A subscription-only monthly online magazine celebrating the "opulence and elegance" of the English language.

Word for Word   <http://plateaupress.com.au/wfw/articles.htm>
Articles on words and phrases by Australian writer Terry O'Connor.

Webliography

Word Fugitives   <http://www.theatlantic.com/unbound/fugitives/>
Barbara Wallraff of the *Atlantic Monthly* features words that ought to exist but don't.

WordOrigins.org   <http://www.wordorigins.org>
Dave Wilton's collection of more than 300 interesting etymologies. Also has a subscription-only monthly newsletter, "A Way With Words."

Verbivore   <http://www.verbivore.com>
Richard Lederer's web site, including excerpts from his popular books on language.

ONLINE DICTIONARIES

American Heritage Dictionary   <http://www.bartleby.com/61/>
The complete text of the 2000 edition, searchable by entry, definition, or full text.

OneLook Dictionaries   <http://www.onelook.com/>
Provides searchable access to a large number of online dictionaries. Multilingual.

Oxford English Dictionary Online   <http://www.oed.com/>
Full access requires a paid subscription, but you can access the Word of the Day and read the regular newsletters free.

YourDictionary.com   <http://www.yourdictionary.com/>
Another collection of dictionary links, to 1800 dictionaries in some 250 languages.

THE LOGOPHILE'S BIBLIOGRAPHY

A Selection of Oxford Dictionaries and Reference Works

DICTIONARIES

The Oxford English Dictionary. Second ed., twenty vols. 1989.

The 500-lb gorilla of the dictionary world, also available online by sub-scription at http://www.oed.com. Check with your local public library to see if they have a subscription for library cardholders available through the library website.

The New Oxford American Dictionary. 2001.

A completely new dictionary of American English from Oxford, with an innovative arrangement of definitions in which the more prominent core senses are given first, with related senses arranged in blocks underneath. This allows for a nice overview of constellations of meaning not possible with other dictionaries. Also available on CD-ROM.

The Oxford American Dictionary and Thesaurus (with Language Guide). 2003.

A very good general dictionary that includes a full thesaurus, plus a great deal of extra usage and language information.

The Concise Oxford Dictionary. Tenth ed. 1999.

The classic desk-size dictionary for British English, including the most current words and phrases and scientific and technical vocabulary. Word

Formation features identify complex word groups such as -*phobias,* -*cultures,* and –*ariums.*

The New Shorter Oxford English Dictionary. Fifth ed., two vols. 2002.
Not just an abridgment of the twenty-volume *OED*, the *Shorter* has its own independent research program. With more than 83,000 quotations, this packs the punch of the *OED*'s literary approach in a more manageable format. Also available on CD-ROM.

DICTIONARIES OF USAGE

Burchfield, R.W. ***The New Fowler's Modern English Usage.*** Third ed. 1996.
A completely revised and expanded version of the beloved *Modern English Usage* with examples from modern authors such as Tom Wolfe, Saul Bellow, and Iris Murdoch.

Fowler, H.W. ***A Dictionary of Modern English Usage.*** Second ed. 1983.
The most-beloved language reference book and the one by which all others are judged. And a darn good read!

Garner, Bryan. ***Garner's Modern American Usage.*** 2003.
The new edition of the classic, from Oxford's authority for American usage. Not just for the grammar-impaired but useful for anyone who would like to write gracefully and precisely.

OTHER WORD BOOKS

Ayto, John. *An A–Z of Food & Drink.* 2002.

The meaning, origin, and development of over 1,200 food and drink terms, plus hundreds of apt food quotations.

Chantrell, Glynnis. *The Oxford Dictionary of Word Histories.* 2002.

This book describes the origins and sense development of over 11,000 words in the English language, with dates of the first recorded evidence from ongoing research for the *OED*.

Delahunty, Andrew, Sheila Dignan, and Penelope Stock. *The Oxford Dictionary of Allusions.* 2001.

A guide to allusions most frequently found in literature both modern and canonical. It covers classical myths and modern culture and ranges from "Ahab" to "Teflon," "Eve" to "Darth Vader." Many entries include a quotation illustrating the allusion in use.

Greenbaum, Sidney. *The Oxford English Grammar.* 1996.

A complete overview of the subject, including a review of modern approaches to grammar and the interdependence of grammar and discourse, word-formation, punctuation, pronunciation, and spelling.

Hargraves, Orin. *Mighty Fine Words and Smashing Expressions.* 2002.

A guide to understanding the stealthy but important differences between American and British English.

Knowles, Elizabeth, ed. *The Oxford Dictionary of Phrase and Fable.* 2000. Drawn from folklore, history, mythology, philosophy, popular culture, religion, science, and technology, these alphabetically arranged entries include ancient gods and goddesses, biblical allusions, proverbial sayings, common phrases, fictional characters, geographical entities, and real people and events.

Lindberg, Christine. *The Oxford American Thesaurus of Current English.* 1999.
A great general thesaurus with an exclusive Writer's Toolkit and more than 350,000 synonyms.

McArthur, Tom. *The Oxford Guide to World English.* 2002.
A fascinating and novel survey of English both as a pre-eminent world language and as an increasingly divergent language.

McKean, Erin. *Weird and Wonderful Words.* 2002. Illustrations by Roz Chast.
Another book just like this one! But with a different 400 weird and wonderful words in it.

Onions, C. T. *The Oxford Dictionary of English Etymology.* 1966.
The standard reference for scholars, this dictionary delves into the origins of more than 38,000 words.